The Iliad Interpreted for E-Commerce

Ego, Rivalry, and the Conflicts That Destroy Online Businesses

ANCIENT WISDOM HACKS

Third Edition

Copyright © 2026 NX, Inc.

Contents

Chapter 2: Achilles' Edge — Crafting an Unbeatable USP

- Why Achilles' Name Terrifies Trojans

- UVP Worksheet & Differentiation Drills

- Copy Formulas & Shield-Style Imagery

- Action Checklist

Chapter 3: The Trojan Horse — Listing That Slips Past Defenses

- Story-First Titles & Headlines That Hook

- Images That Convert & Hidden Warriors

- A+ Content Hacks & Curiosity Flow

- Action Checklist

Chapter 4: Shield Up — Brand Registry & Compliance

- Hoplite Shield Wall: Your IP Armor

Chapter 7: Patroclus' Push — Launch & Early Reviews

Chapter 8: The Embassy — Negotiation Mastery

- Action Checklist

Chapter 9: Zeus-Level Vision — Data & Ads

- PPC Campaign Architecture (Search, Display, Brand)

- Signal Rivers: TACoS, Session %, Glance Views, SOV

- Dashboard Forging & Alerts

- Tactical Cadence: Daily to Monthly Rituals

- Action Checklist

Chapter 10: Night Raid — Competitive Intelligence & Defense

- Monitoring Price Wars, Review Attacks & Hijackers

- Counter-Moves: CS Macros & Automated Defenses

- Psychological Defense: Preventive Narratives

- Action Checklist

Chapter 11: The Ransom of Hector — Customer Service That Calms Rage

- Iliad Lens: Priam Softens Achilles with Empathy

- Empathy Protocol & SLA Targets

- Message Templates & Refund Math

- Turning Returns into Loyalty

- Action Checklist

Chapter 12: Burning Troy — Scaling & Exit

- Multi-Channel Expansion & Brand Bundles

- FBA vs. 3PL Mix & Dynamic Allocation

- Valuation Levers & Due-Diligence Prep

- Broker Checklist & Exit Dance

- Action Checklist

Conclusion & Next Steps — Write Your Own Epic

- Twelve Timeless Principles Recap

- 90-Day War Plan Template

- Glossary of Epic/Amazon Terms

- Further Reading & Resource Links

- Final Call to Arms: Keep Iterating or Be Conquered

Introduction — *Why an Epic for E-commerce?*

1. The Marketplace Is a Battlefield

When Homer opens *The Iliad* he wastes no time naming the real enemy: unbridled, bone-deep competition. "Sing, O goddess, the anger of Achilles son of Peleus, that brought countless ills upon the Achaeans." That single sentence turns a camp of well-armed Greeks into collateral damage the moment pride collides with profit. Switch the shoreline of Troy for Amazon.com and you have today's reality: tens of thousands of sellers compressed onto a single digital beachhead, each certain they've come to win.

It looks cleaner onscreen than bronze against flesh, but the casualty list is real—bank accounts gutted by ads that never convert, brands wiped out by a four-cent price cut, cash flow snapped like a spear shaft when the container ship parks outside Long Beach for three extra weeks. Amazon's Buy Box is a gate that only a few warriors squeeze through at any one moment, and its A-to-Z claims drop like Apollo's arrows when promises aren't met.

Homer's battlefield teaches two non-negotiables. First, violence—physical or algorithmic—is inevitable once limited placement meets unlimited ambition. Second, it's rarely the bigger army that wins; it's the commander who reads the chaos a heartbeat faster. The Greek coalition is larger, but until Achilles re-enters the melee they can only cling to their ships. Likewise, you can pump inventory, PPC spend, and social hype into a product and still watch a nimbler rival overtake you with a smarter bundle image or a timed Lightning Deal.

The poem's grisly detail also reminds us that war is a marathon of nerve endings, not a sprint of biceps. Line after line lists the obscure foot soldiers who pay for a leader's mistake. Sellers see the same pattern when overnight rule changes—battery regulations, pesticide keywords, unexpected hazardous-materials flags—upend months of prep work. One Amazon policy shift equals Apollo loosing another shaft, impartial and lethal.

Yet Homer keeps his camera on leadership choices: Achilles sulks, Hector charges, Agamemnon demands tribute, Odysseus plots. The battle's outcome flows from those decisions, not from fate alone. That's why this book treats the marketplace as a war college rather than a static how-to pane. When you absorb Homer's strategic reflexes, a sudden review attack or unexpected hijacker becomes just another skirmish, not the end of the saga.

---

2. The Characters You'll Meet

Achilles – The Relentless Differentiator
Achilles is raw, undeniable edge. Even his enemies know the math changes when he steps onto the field. After losing Briseis he vows, "Now, therefore, I shall go back to Phthia… for I will not stay here dishonoured to gather gold and substance for you." He'd rather burn opportunity than sell at a discount to someone who devalues him. As a seller, your Achilles moment is brutal focus on

a unique selling proposition—refusing to chase every keyword and instead sharpening the one feature competitors can't copy. But remember Achilles' blind spot: the same intensity that wins also isolates, so pair your differentiator with a supply-chain shield or you'll sit on the sidelines while the war moves on.

Hector – The Guardian of Brand Equity

Hector knows he's mortal yet shoulders the fate of Troy anyway. Andromache pleads, "Husband, this courage of yours dooms you. You show no pity for your little son or your wretched wife…" A brand owner feels that line every time they push more capital into inventory while praying reviews stay five-star. Hector teaches risk management: dual-source, insure shipments, keep an eye on cash burn—fight, but fight with buffers.

He also models resilience. Even when he sees through Athena's trick he squares up: "Death is now indeed exceedingly near at hand… let me first do some great thing that shall be told among men hereafter." Translation for sellers: if the algorithm turns or a black-hat rival steals your images, you still launch a rebuttal video, file those infringement reports, and rally the audience you earned. Going dark is not an option.

Agamemnon – The Aggregator Mind-set

Agamemnon commands by entitlement, not innovation. His reflex is to grab value others created: "You must find me a prize instead, or I alone among the Argives shall be without one." In the marketplace he's the roll-up that scoops brands but forgets product-market fit. Later, with blood rising, he barks, "Let not a man of them be left alive, but let all in Ilius perish, unheeded and forgotten." That's the mindset of a seller who thinks slashing margin to zero will starve competition—and ends up starving their own profit instead. The warning is clear: command scale, yes, but never at the expense of frontline insight.

Odysseus – The Conversion Hacker
 While not front-and-center in Amazon seller lore, Odysseus shows up whenever cunning beats brute force. He's the one who talks Achilles down and slips through Trojan lines at night. His lesson: listings are Trojan horses—visitors must invite you in before they realise you're selling. Every bullet point, image slot, and A+ module must smuggle perceived value past the guards of short attention. Odysseus never swings first; he wins by framing the fight.

Priam – The Voice of Customer Service
 No scene underscores empathy's leverage like Priam kissing the murderous hands of Achilles: "Revere the gods, Achilles! Pity me in my own right, remember your own father!" The hardest-won Prime badge or PPC tweak collapses if you mishandle a refund request. Priam proves that a single, sincere appeal can break even Achilles' rage. Handle tickets with the same humility and speed, and negative feedback becomes a review revision, not a brand obituary.

---

3. Translating Bronze-Age Tactics to Modern Clicks

Ancient spears become ad spend; chariots become 3PLs; the gods themselves morph into algorithms whose motives sellers guess with sacrificial spreadsheets. Yet the underlying combat grammar stays constant.

- **Initiative vs. Reaction.** Achilles' withdrawal lets Hector gain momentum. On Amazon, inertia after stock-out hands ranking to the rival who stayed in stock. Momentum swings are visible in TACoS curves the same way Homer tracks the push and pull along the Scamander.

- **Morale as a Force Multiplier.** When Athena shouts, troops rally; when a leader panics, lines collapse. Your version is brand narrative. A strong mission—"sustainable gear for parents on the go"—turns customers into advocates who defend you in the Q&A and flag knockoffs.

- **Supply Chain = Lines of Communication.** The Greeks fight yards from their ships because logistics is life. Sellers who park everything in FBA without a backup are like warriors who burn their own ships—glorious until the first fire arrow lands.

- **Espionage and Deception.** Odysseus captures Trojan scouts and reverses their intel. You scrape competitor listings, track their coupon timing, and schedule counter-offers that intercept the traffic spike. Same move, just fewer spears.

- **Token Exchange for Goodwill.** Priam's ransom is the world's first white-glove return policy. Modern sellers refund pre-emptively, toss in a free accessory, or upgrade shipping to win back detractors.

Most crucial is the epic's insistence that narrative drives physics. Achilles believes he's wronged, so he pulls out and changes the very weather of war. Likewise, a values-driven origin story inside Brand Story modules lifts conversion more than another ten-percent-off coupon. Story first, tactics second.

---

4. How to Use This Book

Epic poems were recited aloud, giving listeners time to absorb layers of strategy hidden in the verse. You'll use this guide the same way—iteratively, out loud, notebook in hand.

- **Chapter Workflow.** Each of the twelve chapters ends with "Field Orders"—a one-page action checklist. Treat it like a nightly war council. Read the narrative once for insight, then flip straight to the orders and tick boxes while your coffee's still hot.

- **Reread with a Different Helmet.** The first pass as a solopreneur might surface Achilles-level USP tweaks. Six months later, after hiring a VA, reread the Hector sections on delegation and you'll see fresh gaps in your shield wall.

- **Margin Notes.** Homer loved epithet shortcuts—"swift-footed Achilles," "horse-taming Hector." Write your own shorthand next to each tactic: "Ad Blitz," "Coupon Feint," "Branded Bundle." Those tags become the index of your personal epic.

- **Monthly After-Action Review.** At the close of every thirty-day sprint, revisit the conclusion's ninety-day war-plan rubric. Score your niche recon, supply reserves, ad efficiency, and customer sentiment. The rubric forces brutal honesty—the same candor that lets Achilles hurl a spear of words at Agamemnon when he smells hypocrisy.

Remember: an epic is not a sermon but a mirror. Use the quotes as diagnostics. If you start sounding like Agamemnon—complaining about lost spoils before fixing root causes—pause and rewrite your operating cadence. If you drift into Hector's fatal optimism without buffer inventory, reorder sooner. If you ever feel the chill of Achilles' wrath during a review attack, channel it: improve the product, tighten the packaging, sharpen the imaging—then ride out.

---

5. Final Invitation

The Greeks called *kleos* the glory-song echoing after a warrior's death. For sellers, *kleos* isn't a marble statue; it's the screenshot of a customer who says your gadget saved their camping trip, the email from an aggregator offering eight figures, the moment you realise the business can run a week without you.

Homer hands you the archetypes; Amazon hands you the dashboard. This book stitches them together so that every click, coupon, and carton feeds a larger narrative arc. Read aggressively, execute ruthlessly, and—like Achilles sprinting beside the Scamander—never stop moving until your name outlasts the noise.

Chapter 1 – Know the War Before You Sail

Iliad Lens: Achaeans Scout Troy's Walls

On the first dawn after the ships grind onto Trojan sand, the Greek captains stand beneath the battlements and squint upward, reading stonework the way a chess master studies an opening. Homer lingers on the moment before steel meets flesh, when knowledge still outranks courage. "So they sat assembled and spoke together in low voices, peering toward the towering gates of Ilios." In that hush lies the true start of the war. It is not the clash of bronze but the gathering of facts—the ember of strategy that will either kindle victory or leave ashes.

The wall itself is a ledger of insight. Its height tells whether ladders will suffice or siege towers must be built. Arrow slits reveal the defenders' preferred range. The gate count hints at response time: too many and the Trojans can redeploy quickly; too few and their cavalry risks bottleneck. Even the scent of hearth-fires creeping over the parapets whispers the size of stored grain. "For all things speak to the keen-eyed," Odysseus murmurs, "and stone is a tongue to him who listens."

Every seller about to launch on Amazon stands on a similar shoreline. The marketplace rises before you like nine concentric walls of Troy—search results, algorithmic filters, customer reviews, competitor ads, category guidelines, compliance gates, fee

structures, inventory caps, and the invisible architecture of
Amazon's own private motivations. Your first act must mirror the
Achaean scouts: map every rampart before the first arrow flies.

Amazon Lesson: Deep Market Research Beats Blind Launching

A blind launch is the modern equivalent of charging a gate you
have never measured. You may break through by luck; more often
you will bounce, dazed, nursing wounded capital. The point of
reconnaissance is twofold. First, to prove worthy opportunities
exist. Second, to expose silent killers—hidden FBA fees, stubborn
keyword monopolies, review deserts, seasonality dips, patent
tripwires—that could ambush you later.

Think of market research as the song men will sing about your
prudence. Agamemnon ignored warning signs and sparked a
plague among his own ranks. Achilles read every nuance and
chose withdrawal until the time turned ripe. Choose whose
example you emulate.

Niche Recon: Demand, Competition, Margin Heat Map

1. Demand – Hearing the Footfall of the Crowd

Demand is the rumble in the valley before you see the army. On Amazon the vibration manifests as search volume, bestseller rank, and monthly sales estimates. But numbers alone can seduce. A high-volume keyword may be Trojan in disguise, luring novices into a feast-day ambush of price wars and counterfeiters.

Start by harvesting raw search volumes across at least fifty adjacent terms. Imagine each term as a sentry on the wall calling out when shoppers march past. Record three snapshots: current month, same month last year, and three-month average. You are listening for seasonal drumbeats and pandemic-era distortions.

Next, triangulate demand through bestseller rank (BSR) readings on the top twenty organic listings for your primary keyword and for two secondary phrases. BSR is Homer's herald shouting who excels. Capture readings on Monday, Wednesday, Saturday over three consecutive weeks. The fluctuations expose whether sales momentum is steady or artificially inflated through deep-discount blitzes.

Do not stop at raw appetite; measure velocity. Divide each listing's approximate monthly sales by its review count to gauge time-to-trust. If an item racks up 1,000 units per month yet holds 50 reviews, its churn rate dwarfs loyalty; the rampart is thin, ready to crack. Conversely, 400 sales atop 400 reviews suggests a seasoned guard you must outthink, not out-muscle.

2. Competition – Counting the Archers on the Battlements

Competition is not merely headcount; it is discipline, supply lines, and leadership. Inspect page one for telltale markers of entrenched defenders:

- **Brand Share.** How many unique brands command the first three rows? If three players claim twelve slots, they have formed a phalanx.

- **Price Spread.** Note the delta between highest and lowest list price among offers with comparable value propositions. A spread under 20 percent foretells commoditization; a spread over 50 percent signals room for premium positioning or budget incursion.

- **Review Density.** Sum the reviews of the top ten listings, then divide by ten. If the mean sits above 4,000, the walls glimmer with years of arrowheads; a new ladder must be ingenious. Under 500 and you face a lightly guarded outpost.

- **A+ Content Saturation.** Scroll each listing to glimpse enhanced content. Where half or more deploy immersive carousels, the narrative battlefield is already occupied; you must craft an even sharper story or attack through external traffic.

Interpret these metrics together—not in isolation. A niche with monstrous demand and modest review density tempts, but if price spread is razor-thin, margin may evaporate. Conversely, high prices with thick reviews may hide a luxury bastion ripe for a "value-plus" challenger.

3. Margin Heat Map – Where Profit Bleeds or Blossoms

The heat map is your parchment sketch of Troy, colored by feasibility. Construct it row by row:

1. **Landed Cost Estimate.** Sum production quote, inland freight, sea or air freight, import duties, drayage, and final mile to fulfillment center.

2. **FBA Fee Simulation.** Plug dimensions and weight into the latest FBA rate card. Note surcharges for peak season or oversize categories.

3. **Variable Closing and Referral Fees.** Apply category-specific percentages.

4. **Advertising Load.** Forecast cost of advertising as a share of revenue based on keyword CPC benchmarks and your planned TACoS ceiling. Begin conservative at 15 percent; escalate for hypercompetitive categories.

5. **Return and Damage Allowance.** Average return rate for soft goods runs 8 percent; electronics may breach 12 percent. Factor the write-off.

6. **Net Margin.** Subtract all the above from your projected average selling price. Aim for a floor of 20 percent gross margin post-ads if you intend to fund future launches without outside capital.

Plot each product idea along these axes. Those glowing red where margin melts under the sun, discard. Where orange fades to pale green, proceed to advanced scouting—sample orders, inspection, packaging prototypes. Where margins blaze emerald, circle twice: these may be deceptively fertile, drawing rival kings, so ensure your differentiators are durable.

Above all, remember Hector's warning that courage without caution ruins families. Your heat map is the pact you make with Andromache that Troy will not lose its prince to vanity.

Keyword Trench Maps: Tools & Methods

The Spartans fought shoulder-to-shoulder because gaps killed. Keywords form your trenches, and any gap leaks clicks to the enemy. While demand and competition tell you whether to wage war, keyword mapping dictates how.

1. Gathering Seed Phrases – The Initial Probe

Begin with a list of five to ten baseline phrases you believe customers use. For a collapsible water bottle these might be "foldable water bottle," "travel water flask," "silicone bottle," and so on. Enter each into an all-in-one tool—Helium 10, Jungle Scout, DataDive—recording exact-match search volume, competing ASIN count, and top-five click-share percentage.

Avoid the temptation to indulge only large volumes. Achilles strikes at Hector, not every shield-bearer. Low-volume but hyper-relevant phrases often cost pennies per click, letting you trench deeper under cover of budgetary night.

2. Lateral Expansion – Echoes Along the Wall

Next generate lateral variants: color terms ("black collapsible bottle"), size descriptors ("750 ml"), material cues ("BPA-free"), usage context ("hiking water bottle foldable"). Feed each variant back through your tool. The goal is not to hoard words but to trace tributaries of intent.

Examine two key ratios:

- **Search Volume to PPC Bid Ratio.** A high volume paired with moderate bids is fertile trench territory—like soft clay to carve bunkers.

- **Search Volume to Relevance Score.** Some tools grade how closely a phrase matches the seed. High volume yet low relevance can siphon ad budget without conversion, much like arrows loosed at shadows.

Retain phrases that score at least medium relevance and do not exceed your target bid threshold. You are shaping the front line, not scattering troops.

3. Deep Vertical – Drilling Under the Walls

Now pivot to long-tail phrases, three to six words in length. These are Trojan postern gates seldom guarded. Use Amazon's autocomplete to harvest suggestions. Type slowly: "collapsible water bottle for …," "foldable flask leak proof …." Each completion is a whispered rumor of need. Record them.

Equip a reverse-ASIN lookup against the top five competitors. Filter their converting phrases by search volume tier—low, medium, high—and remove duplicates you already own. What remains are arrow slits they occupy that you have not yet noticed.

For each phrase compute:

- **Organic Ranking Difficulty.** If three or more listings with under 100 reviews rank in the top ten, the gate is weak.

- **Click-to-Conversion Disparity.** If the phrase enjoys strong volume yet competitors' listing titles lack an exact match, there is unclaimed keyword real estate in copywriting.

Add these priority phrases to a "first-week ranking" list. Your initial PPC and content strategy will hammer them until you penetrate those slits.

4. Cartography – Building the Trench Map

Visualize your keywords as concentric rings around the main gate. Core ring: high-volume, main intent phrases worthy of title placement. Middle ring: mid-volume modifiers suitable for bullet points, A+ headings, image alt text, and top-of-search campaigns. Outer ring: long-tails for back-end search terms, auto campaigns, and defensive exact-match ads at low bids.

Sketch the rings on paper or mind-mapping software. Annotate each phrase's CPC, conversion rate, and your current organic rank. This evolving diagram becomes your daily morning briefing—the same parchment Odysseus unrolls to show which sally ports to torch at dusk.

5. Maintaining the Trenches – Rhythm of Recon

Reconnaissance is not a pre-battle chore but a rhythm. Schedule bi-weekly keyword audits: extract search term reports, sort by spend-without-sales, and plug leaks by negating or lowering bids. Promote breakthroughs by raising budgets where conversion outpaces cost.

Watch seasonality. A phrase like "back-to-school water bottle" surges in August; widen the trench early July. In winter, "ski hydration bottle" flickers; decide if it justifies a temporary outpost. As the months roll, you will see your map shimmer like heat waves—learn to read that shimmer as sure as Ajax senses a flank opening.

Action Checklist

- Stand on the shoreline before you order samples. Capture demand, competition, and margin for at least **three** candidate niches, comparing snapshots over multiple weeks.

- Assemble a **landed-cost worksheet** that leaves nothing blank: production, freight, import duty, inspection, packaging, FBA intake. Adjust for currency risk if paying suppliers in RMB or EUR.

- Draft your **margin heat map** and kill any idea that cannot survive at 20 percent post-ad margin under worst-case TACoS.

- Harvest **fifty seed keywords**. Expand laterally and vertically until you maintain a list of at least **200 phrases** sorted into core, middle, outer rings.

- Build your **keyword trench map** on paper or digital canvas; review it every morning during launch month and weekly thereafter.

- Schedule **bi-weekly audits** of search term reports; negate non-converting queries, raise bids on profitable conversions, and move breakthrough phrases from outer to middle ring.

- Keep a **war journal**. Record insights, price shifts, CPC spikes, review anomalies. History is the truest teacher; yesterday's battle notes guard tomorrow's victory.

Closing Reflection

When the scouts returned to Agamemnon, they did not bring poetry. They carried counts of gatehouses, thickness of timber, guard rotations. Those dry facts became the breath of strategy.

Likewise, every spreadsheet you compile, every CPC you log, every margin you calculate may feel mundane beside the lure of branding shots and influencer reels. But in the end it is these numbers—stone-solid, wall-high—that decide whether your flag flies above Troy or drifts ashore among splintered oars.

Listen again to the epic voice: "But the wise captains weighed every sign, and from each silent stone they read the fate of spears." Read your marketplace just as fiercely. Know the war before you sail, and the moment your prow cuts the algorithmic surf, you will do so with the calm of a commander who already owns tomorrow's dawn.

Chapter 2 – Achilles' Edge — Crafting an Unbeatable USP

1. Iliad Lens: Why Achilles' Name Alone Terrifies Trojans

When Homer first lets Achilles loose, the earth itself seems to flinch. "But when the son of Peleus rose, the Trojans saw and their knees were loosened, and the heart of each man shook." Notice that nothing has happened yet—no spear thrown, no shield shattered. Fear erupts at the **name** alone. Hector calls him "that man who makes all hearts sink," and even the river Scamander, a god in its own right, begs him to stand down. Achilles embodies a principle every Amazon seller must master: **distinctive identity beats mere presence**.

His edge is not just strength; dozens of Achaean warriors swing heavy bronze. What magnifies Achilles is the **full stack of differentiation**:

- **Origin Story:** Son of a goddess, dipped in immortal water.

- **Visible Marker:** The blazing Shield of Hephaestus, a mobile legend in bronze.

- **Audible Signal:** War cry compared to "a trumpet blaring death."

- **Unmatched Performance:** He outruns rivers, out-duels champions, and slays "so many men that the banks of the stream are crowded."

- **Reputation Cycle:** Each fresh exploit loops back into rumor. Panic spreads before he arrives, tilting contests in advance.

Brand that into your mind. On Amazon, your product is one tile among sixty on a phone screen. Unless customers **recognize and believe** your edge before they click, price decides. Achilles never lets combat reduce to arithmetic; his legend warps the math. Your Unique Value Proposition (UVP) must do the same.

---

2. The UVP Mind-Set — Bleeding Out the Generic

Most listings drown in adjectives—"premium, durable, perfect"—none worth remembering. A UVP slices through that muck like Achilles through the Trojan rank, concise and final. To forge it, you answer three questions with knife-sharp clarity:

1. **Who exactly is this for?**

2. **What problem does it solve or desire does it satisfy more completely than anything else?**

3. **Why should the buyer trust that claim on sight?**

If any answer feels padded, the edge dulls. In the poem, Trojans never wonder **who** Achilles serves, **what** he can do, or **why** he can do it. The evidence precedes him.

---

3. UVP Worksheet — From Myth to Mechanism

Use the following steps like smithy blows on molten ore. Write by hand if possible; physical movement slows thought, forcing precision.

Step 1: Nail the Hero & Foe
Hero = Your customer segment in eleven words or fewer: "Trail-running parents who carry toddlers."
Foe = The pain agitating them: "Bulk water bottles that leak and hog pack space."

Step 2: Map Stakes
Describe the daily cost if the foe wins—wet gear, cranky child, ruined hike. Include emotional vocabulary: annoyance, anxiety, embarrassment.

Step 3: Declare the Fatal Blow
Spell the one feature or outcome that annihilates that pain. Example: "Bottle shrinks to palm-size disc in three folds."

Step 4: Forge Proof
Pick at least two of these and draft hard evidence for each:
Quantified test, third-party rating, patent or patent pending, origin story, authority testimonial, lab certification, before-after photo set.

Step 5: Compress to a Battle-Cry

Push the parts into a headline no longer than 15 words:

> "Palm-Fold Bottle—gear-dry confidence for
> trail-running parents, lab-tested 100% leak-proof."

Recite aloud. If it fails to stick after three repetitions, re-forge.

---

4. Differentiation Drills — Tempering the Edge

A claim is brittle until tempered against rivals. Repeat these drills until sparks fly.

Drill A: The Ten-Scroll Gauntlet

Scroll the search results for your primary keyword ten screen lengths deep. For each competing title, jot its main promise. Now highlight any promise identical to yours. If four or more overlap, your edge is blunt. Change the metal: add an exclusive accessory, upgrade material grade, extend warranty, or bundle digital training. Re-test.

Drill B: The Achilles Heel Test

Achilles is nearly invincible, yet the text never hides his heel. Identify your own potential heel **before** competitors shoot arrows: long lead times, fragile colorways, painful unboxing. Craft counters—local micro-stock, reinforced packaging, magnetic open tab—then brag about them in copy so no rival can weaponize the weakness.

Drill C: The Hector-Proof Endurance Run

Hector endures far longer than expected because he masters stamina. Simulate a six-month ad war in a spreadsheet: inflate CPC by 40 percent, assume two unexpected stock-outs, and slash conversion by 15 percent to mimic a review hit. Does margin survive? If not, refine cost of goods or raise price until it does. Otherwise your edge dulls under sustained siege.

Drill D: The Scamander Shock

Achilles fights a literal river. Test your product in an environment harsher than typical use—freeze, drop, overfill. Record footage. Surviving that ordeal converts skeptics faster than any bullet point. Show, do not tell.

---

5. Copy Formulas — Turning Edge into Language

Great copy is the herald running ahead of Achilles, shouting doom. Use formulas, then add voice.

Formula 1: Problem-Agitate-Obliterate

Problem: "Water bottles leak. Packs soak. Days ruin."
Agitate: "Mid-hike clothes squelch, toddler fusses, and you smell plastic taste for miles."

Obliterate: "Palm-Fold's triple-seal lid slams leaks shut—shake it, drop it, trust it."

Place this in the first two bullets.

Formula 2: Feature-Advantage-Meaning

Feature: "Collapses to 1-inch disc."
Advantage: "Frees 80 percent of pack volume."
Meaning: "Carry snacks, first-aid, or just lighter shoulders."

Buyers skim; this structure lets them land anywhere yet grasp the why.

Formula 3: Authority-Story-Invitation

Authority: "Certified food-grade silicone, SGS report available."
Story: "Inspired by a climber-dad who cut weight after a summit scare."
Invitation: "Join 40,000 parents who refuse heavy gear—add to cart now."

Authority calms doubt, story sparks empathy, invitation channels energy into purchase.

Formula 4: Rhythmic Repetition

Homer wields epithets to brand characters: "swift-footed Achilles," "horse-taming Hector." Choose one rhythmic tag for your product and echo it across images, A+ headers, and package insert. Example: "Pack-Light Power." Repetition cements memory.

6. Imagery & Design — The Shield of Hephaestus Principle

Achilles' shield is a narrative unto itself: constellations, harvest scenes, rivers, and cities engraved in concentric rings. It mesmerizes foes before deflecting spears. Translate that into listing imagery:

- **Hero Image:** Command the page with a bold silhouette; no clutter, immaculate lighting, slight angle to suggest motion.

- **Ring 1 — Functional Panels:** Infographic showing the core mechanism: folding stages, leak test, size comparison next to a smartphone.

- **Ring 2 — Lifestyle Panels:** User scenarios—trail, stroller walk, airport line—mirroring the customer's aspirational self.

- **Ring 3 — Proof Panels:** Lab test snapshot, warranty badge, patent number. Facts slice through skepticism.

- **Ring 4 — Origin Panel:** Founder photo, 60-word tale of invention at 4,000 meters altitude. Story glows at the rim, just like the harvest scenes on the shield's edge.

7. Pricing the Edge — Terror Before Contact

Achilles never haggles; his demand is implicit. Price must signal your edge before shoppers zoom the thumbnail. Three principles:

1. **Anchor at a Premium:** Start higher than the category's median plus 10 percent. Signal that you are not generic.

2. **Justify in Copy & Kit:** Bundle value extras—carabiner clip, digital hydration tracker—worth at least 30 percent of perceived price.

3. **Hold Line for Forty-Five Days:** Resist discounting until reviews cross your social-proof threshold. Cutting price early bleeds mystique.

Remember, Trojans felt dread **from afar**. Price is the modern aura; wield it.

---

8. Launch Mechanics — Turning Name into Momentum

Achilles' first charge creates a vacuum; Trojan lines fold; momentum cascades. Your launch must echo that surge:

- **Day-1 Micro-Tribe:** Seed twenty units to hand-picked superfans in exchange for brutally honest feedback, not incentivized reviews. Their social media noise primes the algorithm.

- **Day-3 Exact-Match Blitz:** Run exact-match ads on ten long-tail phrases from your core. Bid to top of search for seven days. Early sales train Amazon to link your ASIN with your claim.

- **Day-10 Review Fuse:** Trigger request-a-review sequence; follow with a customer-service check-in that *serves* not pushes. Achilles does not beg; he earns fear.

- **Day-15 Shield-Wall Price:** Maintain premium price, but add a tick-box coupon worth 5 percent. The flank is protected—perceived deal without eroding anchor.

- **Day-30 Story Echo:** Drop a founder-story video in Brand Story module. Pair with a brand-registered ad spot showing the thumbnail plus tagline. Keep messaging laser-consistent.

Momentum, once rolling, smothers cheaper rivals who need twice the volume to match ranking signals.

---

9. Action Checklist

- Complete the UVP worksheet: Hero, Foe, Stakes, Fatal Blow, Proof, Battle-Cry.

- Run the Ten-Scroll Gauntlet; if four or more titles share your promise, tweak product or positioning.

- Identify your **heel**; design countermeasures and boast about them in imagery.

- Stress-test margin with the Hector-Proof six-month model. Adjust COGS or price until profits endure a 40 percent CPC surge.

- Film the Scamander Shock demo; embed it as second image and pin preview on video ad.

- Craft headline using Problem-Agitate-Obliterate. Write five versions; choose the punchiest.

- Develop rhythmic epithet (e.g., "Pack-Light Power"). Insert in title, first bullet, image ALT text, and package insert.

- Design shield-style image set: hero, functional, lifestyle, proof, origin.

- Anchor price at category median + 10 percent; hold firm forty-five days.

- Execute Day-1 micro-tribe seeding, Day-3 ad blitz, Day-15 coupon, Day-30 story echo.

- Review metrics weekly: organic rank for core keywords, review velocity, ACOS vs. TACOS, share of voice.

- Log insights in war journal; iterate product V2 by week
  eight.

---

10. Closing Charge

Homer writes: "Sweeping on like a flame of fire, Achilles fell upon
the Trojans." The flame burned because wood—his legend—was
dry and ready long before the spark. Your unbeatable USP is that
dry tinder. By the time a shopper lands on your page, their mind
should flicker: "Of course I choose this; everything else feels
lesser." If doubt remains, your edge is blunt. Sharpen again. Keep
forging until your very name loosens knees in the search results.
Then, and only then, sail for Troy.

Chapter 3 – The Trojan Horse — Listing That Slips Past Defenses

1. The Metaphor Unpacked — Cunning in the Click Age

The Iliad closes before the Trojans drag that fatal horse inside their gates, yet Homer sprinkles the seeds of the plot in his constant praise of "resourceful Odysseus." Late in the war, when Agamemnon falters, Odysseus answers, "I will steal into their councils, set snares in their ways, and leave them no heart for battle." That vow foreshadows the hollow beast that will smuggle Greeks past every spear point.

E-commerce defenses are less bloody but just as real: ad blindness, price filters, default sort, and dopamine-numbed thumbs. A shopper's guard rises the instant the page loads, scanning for tricks. An ordinary listing charges straight at that wall and is repelled by scrolls and swipes. The Trojan Horse strategy flips the assault: invite the customer to open the gate voluntarily, then conquer doubt from the inside with proof, story, and desire.

2. Story-First Titles — The First Wheel Over the Drawbridge

The Trojans did not drag the horse close because it looked like a war machine. They saw a narrative of "an offering to the gods, a plea for safe passage home" etched into the timber. Without that story carved in letters taller than a spear, the wheels would have sunk in the sand.

Your title is the carved inscription. Amazon allows roughly 200 characters, but only the first fifty display on mobile before truncation. Those fifty must whisper lore. Start with the core keyword, yes—Odysseus still needed it called a "horse" so scouts could report honestly—but immediately splice in narrative fragments that spark emotion or curiosity:

- **Tension Phrase:** what is lost without your product.

- **Resolution Phrase:** the unique rescue you offer.

Example:

> "Collapsible Water Bottle for Trail-Running Parents – Palm-Fold Design Ends Leaks Forever."

The first phrase aligns with search intent ("collapsible water bottle"), ensuring the sentries allow closer inspection. The dash functions like Odysseus' carved plea. The second phrase ("Palm-Fold Design Ends Leaks Forever") flips the mind from evaluation to intrigue: *How can folding end leaks?*—click.

To forge your own inscription, test these three chisels:

1. **Mythic Allusion:** a single bold word that paints an image: "Titan-Grade," "Feather-Light," "Bullet-Proof."

2. **Specific Salvation:** a measured promise: "Stays Cold 24 Hrs," "No-Skip Pages," "Connects in 3 Sec."

3. **Buyer Identity:** a quick nod to who will benefit: "for Busy Baristas," "for Tiny Apartments," "for Marathon Moms."

Blend two of the three; never all three, or the timber looks crowded and inauthentic.

---

3. Images That Convert — The Hidden Warriors

Once the gates swing inward, soldiers must leap out fast; the shopper must see proof before adrenaline cools. Images are those warriors. They fight in a strict order of battle:

Frame 1 — The Hero Shot

A horse that looked flimsy would have been torched outside the rampart. Your hero image must arrest the feed with clarity and gravity. Use a single, shadow-free angle on a pure backdrop, no props, the product filling 85 percent of the frame. If color variants exist, lead with the boldest hue, even if the neutral tones outsell later; boldness is your flag in the distance.

Frame 2 — The Instant Proof

Greek craftsmen hid bronze plate inside the horse. Reveal your plating with a crisp infographic: arrows pointing to the hinge, the seal, the button. Overlay a concise boast: "100% Leak-Proof Seal – Lab Verified." Shoppers trust images faster than text; the promise lodges before skepticism loads.

Frame 3 — The Commanding Context

Zoom out: show the bottle clipped to a runner's waistband in mid-stride, water beads frozen mid-air. Context validates scale and lifestyle. Keep background uncluttered so the hero object still dominates.

Frame 4 — The Pain Contrast

Split the frame: left half a soaked backpack sagging, right half dry gear next to the folded bottle. Humans process contrasts instantly. The brain asks, *Which side of the gate will I stand on?*

Frame 5 — The Credibility Crest

Display certifications, patent numbers, warranty period. Arrange them like shields on a wall, small but unmistakable. Achilles' shield was a story in metal; this frame is your micro-epic of authority.

Frame 6 — The Narrative Close

Founder photographed in natural setting—trail overlook at dawn—holding product. Caption beneath: "I designed Palm-Fold after a ridge hike ended with my toddler shivering under a damp jacket." A face anchors emotion; the story circles back to the title's promise.

Frame 7+ — Optional Reels and GIFs

If video is approved, a 15-second loop showing fold-fill-shake with bounce tests quadruples retention. Keep text overlays minimal. The viewer's subconscious must sense durability and delight without reading.

---

4. A+ Content Hacks — Loading the Inner Keep

Once inside the city center, the Greeks still had to navigate alleys to open the main gates for their fleet. A+ Content (or Premium A+ if unlocked) is that city center. Default product descriptions resemble cramped passages; A+ widens lanes into immersive persuasion that correlates with conversion lifts up to 10 percent.

Hack 1: The Scrolling Saga

Structure modules like acts:

- **Act I — The Oath:** a three-column banner stating pain, quest, breakthrough.

- **Act II — The Trials:** carousel of torture tests: freeze, drop, crush. Each slide stamped with a bold verb: "Freeze," "Drop," "Crush."

- **Act III — The Boon:** full-width lifestyle image flanked by a pull quote from a verified review.

- **Act IV — The Fellowship:** a grid of companion products gating a bundle purchase or multi-ASIN cross-sell.

This rhythm mimics oral storytelling: problem, struggle, victory, return. Keep each act scroll-level distinct, so thumbs feel progress like chapters.

Hack 2: The Story Aperture Technique

Begin A+ with a banner where text covers only twenty percent of the image on the left, leaving a vast uncluttered right side that draws the eye forward. Amazon's platform dims images on half-scroll; the empty space becomes a beckoning road, urging further scroll.

Hack 3: The Reversal Caption

Under each photo, start with a negative word that flips to a positive: "Heavy? Never." "Leaks? Impossible." Micro-contrast jolts the inattentive brain awake one extra beat.

Hack 4: Hidden SEO Reservoir

Embed synonyms and long-tail phrases in image alt-text—Amazon reads them for indexing. Do not cram; two per image suffices. It's the whisper under the horse's belly: invisible but potent.

Hack 5: The Velvet FAQ Trapdoor

At the bottom, include a collapsible FAQ with the most
destabilizing objections: "Will the hinge wear out?" "Is silicone safe
when frozen?" Answer with crisp engineering evidence. The
collapsible format smooths scroll friction; only the doubtful open it,
and when they do, trust spikes.

---

5. Psychological Triggers — Lessons from the Horse Applied to Flow

The horse succeeded because it exploited five mental levers:
authority, scarcity, reciprocity, curiosity, and inevitability. Each
maps directly onto listing elements.

Authority

The horse arrived stamped with Athena's supposed blessing.
Authority on Amazon equals high review count, third-party tests,
trademarks, and professional imagery. Deploy authority
early—second image, first bullet—so the guard relaxes.

Scarcity

Trojan priest Laocoön warned, "Whatever it is, I fear the Greeks,
even when they bring gifts." He feared *because* the gift was
singular. On your page, limited-time coupons, low stock badges, or
limited-edition colorways generate urgency. Use sparingly; scarcity
becomes noise if omnipresent.

Reciprocity

The horse was framed as a tribute after the Greeks "paid for their flight with tears." Offer immediate reciprocity by bundling a digital asset: an e-book, recipe pack, or tutorial. Free value flips the consumer from guarded to grateful, nudging purchase.

Curiosity

Why a horse? Why so large? Curiosity pulled the Trojans closer. Trigger it in your listing flow: reveal part of the mechanism in the title, more in the hero image, full explanation in image 2, and live demo only once they click video. The mind chases closure.

Inevitability

Once inside, the war was functionally over. Your listing must march the buyer toward a sense that purchase is inevitable. Align bullets in problem-solution hierarchy, end each with a mini-call-to-action that escalates: "Pack lighter; hike farther; add to cart now." The cart button becomes the drawbridge lever—one last pull clears all debate.

---

6. Modern Listing Flow — The Night Opened

Combine every element into a choreographed path that matches the brain's scanning habit.

1. **Search Results Tile**: Title's hook plus striking hero image.

2. **Top-of-Fold**: Price, rating, coupon badge, bullet one summarizing UVP in a single bold phrase.

3. **Image Gallery Rapid-Swipe**: Proof, context, pain contrast, narrative close—all loaded, each under 2 MB for swift rendering.

4. **Bullets Deep-Dive**: Five bullets following Problem-Agitate-Obliterate and Feature-Advantage-Meaning blends. Use inline caps: "NO-SPILL," "TSA-READY."

5. **A+ Story Saga**: Acts I–IV as above, culminating in cross-sell grid.

6. **Review Pit**: Showcase a pinned top review with images and a short reply from brand founder; humanize the echo chamber.

7. **FAQ Trapdoor**: Objections neutralized.

8. **Add-On Upsell**: "Buy with Palm-Fold Filter Kit" box surfaces just before the "Customers also viewed" moat where rivals lurk.

A shopper tumbling through this flow experiences micro-wins: curiosity met, doubt eased, aspiration fed. By the time external ads and competitors appear, loyalty has already stowed away inside their conviction.

7. Action Checklist

- **Title Forge**: Draft five story-first titles. Speak each aloud. Keep one that sticks after a ten-minute break.

- **Image Lineup**: Shoot or render the seven-frame warrior sequence. Audit for glare, color accuracy, text legibility at 50 percent zoom.

- **A+ Architecture**: Sketch Acts I–IV on paper, listing the hero image, headline, sub copy. Build in Amazon module sandbox before pushing live.

- **Alt-Text Plan**: Assign two long-tail keywords per image. Verify uniqueness.

- **Authority Vault**: Gather certificates, lab reports, press quotes. Overlay badges on frame five; store PDFs in brand storefront for one-click proof.

- **Scarcity Trigger**: Schedule first tick-box coupon to run three days per month. Disable when stock dips below 15 percent.

- **Reciprocity Asset**: Write or commission a 1,500-word quick-start guide PDF. Deliver via post-purchase email with neutral language, no review request.

- **Curiosity Trail**: Insert cliff-hanger wording in bullet one; expand in image 2 caption; finale in A+ Act II.

- **FAQ Drilling**: List top ten support tickets from competitors' reviews. Draft conscientious answers for each; collapse into FAQ module.

- **Review Spotlight**: Tag a customer image review that depicts product in extreme use. Respond publicly, thanking with a tip, not a discount.

- **Flow Audit**: On mobile, time the scroll from hero image to Add-On Upsell. Aim for under 55 seconds. Trim copy if slower.

- **Journal Reflection**: After thirty days, note conversion rate swing versus pre-A+ era. Correlate with ad spend and review velocity. Adjust.

---

8. Closing Torchlight

Night falls; the Trojans sleep; the horse's hatch opens. Odysseus steps onto the courtyard stones and whispers to his companions, "Now is the hour—neither too soon, lest they be roused, nor too late, lest the dawn unmask us." Timing, stealth, and narrative convergence: every element perfected before a sword is drawn.

Your listing must practice the same nocturnal art. It enters under escort of keywords, displays humble homage to the customer's need, then unpacks layers of trust until resistance fades. Only then does it unsheathe the final call to action, clear and fearless: **Buy Now**.

Remember Odysseus' boast to Achilles early in the epic: "You may be stronger, but I claim to be the better strategist." Strength in e-commerce is budget, ranking, scale; strategy is listing alchemy. Build your horse with precision, hide your finest arguments within, and wheel it beneath the soaring gates of search. While rivals still batter the walls with discounts and hashtags, your standard will already be flying over the captured city—victory won in silence before the first light of dawn.

Chapter 4 – Shield Up — Brand Registry & Compliance

1. Iliad Lens — The Hoplite Wall and the Meaning of a Shield

Homer gives us one of literature's tightest phalanx portraits when he writes, "Like the close-set stones of a towering wall they stood, shield overlapping shield, helmet touching helmet, every crest a brother to the next." The power of the Greek hoplite barrage was never the brilliance of one warrior but the interlock—iron lips kissing iron, no daylight for an arrow. When Ajax plants his tower-shield in the dust, Menelaus slides his own beside it; Achilles could sprint far ahead, yet even he knows a moment arrives when speed must yield to formation.

On Amazon the phalanx is legal protection. Your trademark, your design patent, your compliance paperwork—each a bronze plate. Alone they fend off a few blows; locked together they form a wall that repels wholesalers impersonating you, sellers who "borrow" your images, factories that reroute your molds to back-door listings, and the algorithmic plague of inauthentic claims.

Without that wall, commerce reverts to chaos. The Trojan prince Pandarus snaps his bowstring at the truce, and an arrow slips between the harness plates of Menelaus, throwing the entire battlefield back into blood. One lapse, one empty gap in your IP defense, and rivals pour through. The remainder of this chapter is a shield-smith's forge—step-by-step blows that bend raw filings of paperwork into armor bright enough to blind counterfeiters before they loose their shafts.

---

2. Trademarks — The Central Boss of the Shield

The round shield's heart is the **boss**, the raised dome that deflects the direct strike. Your registered trademark is that boss: the single most recognized, legally enforceable symbol of ownership.

2.1. Choosing a Mark Worth Defending

A strong mark is **distinctive** (invented or arbitrary words like "Kodak" or "Apple" for computers) rather than descriptive ("FoldBottle") or generic ("Collapsible Bottle"). "Swift-footed Achilles" is memorable because no other warrior shares the epithet; so must your brand name stand apart in the trademark register.

Avoid crowded classes. Before investing in logos, run a Basic Word Mark search in the USPTO database and the EUIPO TMview for your core product class (International Class 21 for drinkware, for example). A hit list of near-identicals means the parade ground is already shoulder-to-shoulder—change your flag now or forever share the field.

2.2. Filing Fundamentals

A standard character mark covers any stylization of the words. A design mark protects the logo shape. File both if budget allows; if not, start with word mark—easier to enforce in text-only infringement (title, bullet point, PPC hijacks).

Key inputs:

- Owner entity name and address.

- Exact wording.

- International classes (stick to classes that mirror actual or imminent product lines).

- Specimen: photo of product or packaging actually in commerce.

Choose **TEAS Plus** for lower fee, but commit to strict formatting. The moment USPTO accepts your serial number, you wield a provisional blade. Full registration may take 8–12 months; you do not stand idle—Amazon Brand Registry can unlock once your application is filed, as we shall see.

3. Design Patents — Carving Your Shield Rim

A design patent guards the **ornamental morphology** of your product—curves, ridges, hinge pattern. Think of Achilles' shield, described in layers of city scenes, shepherd dances, swirling ocean. No craftsman could replicate that relief without infringing the immortal smith Hephaestus.

3.1. Is Your Shape Patent-Worthy?

Design protection requires novelty and non-obviousness. A foldable bottle may be common, but if your hinge pattern forms a spiral never before seen, you wield novelty. Compile an **inspiration board** of current marketplace shapes; mark every space you deviate.

3.2. Speed to File

Sketches suffice; you do not need final molds. File a provisional application (low cost, buys twelve months) to stamp the invention date. Convert to non-provisional within that window with a professional set of drawings—six orthogonal views plus perspective.

3.3. Global Reach

The Hague System lets you extend coverage to 90+ territories in one filing. Target first the locales that pump copycats into Amazon—China, Europe, Canada. Just as the hoplite carries a shield width ample to guard his neighbor's left side, your design patent should span enough markets to cover flanks you have yet to exploit.

---

4. Amazon Brand Registry — Locking Shields Edge to Edge

With a serial number or registration in hand, march to **Brand Registry**. In Homeric terms, it is the moment your Helepolis—the city-taking machine—rolls forward.

4.1. Eligibility Recap

- Active text-based or image-based trademark in each territory where you enroll.

- Matching brand name permanently affixed to product or packaging.

- Amazon account in good standing (no unresolved intellectual-property violations).

4.2. Enrollment Steps

1. Log into Seller Central.

2. Navigate to Brand Registry portal; submit brand name, trademark office, registration or application number.

3. Provide images of product and packaging showing the trademark.

4. Verify via code sent to trademark correspondent email.

Approval can occur in 24 hours if documentation is pristine.

4.3. Immediate Weapons

Brand Registry is more than a badge. It grants:

- **Brand Dashboard** with real-time infringement alerts.

- **A+ Content** and **Brand Story** modules (already leveraged in Chapter 3).

- **Sponsored Brand Ads** and **Video Ads**—premium placements your copycat cannot buy.

- **Project Zero** self-service takedown (once you build a 90-day record of correct infringement submissions).

Like interlocked shields, each feature overlaps another's weak spot. A fraudster swaps your photos? Visual combat tools let you report. Hijacker lists under your brand? Transparency codes (see below) break their supply chain.

5. Amazon IP Accelerator — Forging Faster with a God-Smith

Achilles' armor is delivered overnight from divine smithy. You, too, can accelerate. **IP Accelerator** connects you with vetted law firms who file and docket your trademark in days, plus unlock Brand Registry within two weeks of filing.

5.1. Cost vs. Time

Expect $600–$900 legal fee plus USPTO filing fee ($250 per class). Compare that to DIY: $250 fee but weeks of learning forms. The lost weeks keep your listing naked against duplicates. In high-piracy categories—electronics accessories, beauty—IP Accelerator is the spear that arrives just before the ambush.

5.2. Global Footprint

IP Accelerator now spans Canada, Mexico, Brazil, UK, EU, India. File simultaneously in each and Brand Registry toggles on in local marketplaces automatically. If Troy has many gates, break them all in one night.

---

6. Counterfeit Patrol — Scout Lines Beyond the Ditch

The wall protects only what you can see. Patrols ride the plain at dawn to spot siege engines under construction. Modern patrol is a stack of programs and habits.

6.1. Transparency — Serializing the Shield

Enrolling in **Transparency** adds a unique QR-style code to every unit you manufacture. Amazon scans the code inbound at its FC and again outbound to the customer. Units without valid codes are blocked. No code, no sale. For your supplier, it introduces logistical friction that discourages siphoning extra production to gray markets.

6.2. Project Zero — One-Click Arrows

Once your accuracy rate on infringement claims exceeds 90 percent over three months, Amazon grants **Project Zero** status: you delete infringing ASINs instantly, bulk or single. No waiting for Seller Support; no war councils; one arrow shot. Use sparingly and only for genuine violations—abuse triggers penalties and shrinks your strategic bandwidth.

6.3. Automated Brand Protections

Amazon's algorithm flags suspect listings that use your trademark in titles or bullets. Enable Brand Registry's **automated protections**; review flagged ASINs daily. Accept legitimate resellers; annihilate impostors.

6.4. Off-Platform Sweep

Counterfeits spawn on eBay, Walmart, Facebook Marketplace, Shopee. Set a monthly crawl routine: search your brand plus keywords "cheap," "replica," "authentic" with minus filters to exclude your own store links. Use VeRO (eBay), Brand Portal

(Meta), and DMCA takedowns. Victory in one theater means
nothing if another flank burns.

---

7. Compliance Trenches — Safety, Labeling, and the Gods of Bureaucracy

Homer's warriors fear Zeus more than spears; sellers must
appease regulators. A product that lacks required certifications
can be de-listed overnight, shredding the entire phalanx from
within.

7.1. General Product Safety Regulations

- **CPSC / CPSIA** for children's products: Lead, phthalates,
  small-parts testing, tracking labels.

- **FDA** for food-contact items: 21 CFR 177.2600 (silicone
  elastomers), testing for extractables.

- **Prop 65** for California exposure warnings (lead, BPA,
  DEHP).

Compile a compliance dossier: lab reports, declarations of
conformity, safety data sheets. Store digitally in a **compliance
vault** folder; Amazon can demand within 48 hours.

7.2. Labeling

Map every surface that must carry information: importer name, address, trademark, country of origin, batch code, safety icons, choking hazard. Laser-etch or mold these labels—stickers peel, and a peeled sticker equals suspended listing.

7.3. Documentation on Seller Central

Under **Manage Compliance**, pre-upload docs against SKU. Amazon's automated checks run quietly; you avoid future "Documents Required" red-flag bulletins that cripple sales mid-quarter.

---

8. Enforcement Playbook — Spears Over the Rampart

Even the best wall sees arrows lofted over. Be ready to strike back.

8.1. Cease and Desist

Draft a templated letter citing trademark registration number, infringing ASIN, and demanded action deadline (48 hours). Send via Amazon messaging and public email. A surprising percentage retreat immediately when confronted with registration proof.

8.2. Infringement Report

Inside Brand Registry, file under **Report a Violation**. Choose type: trademark, counterfeit, copyright, patent. Attach side-by-side images and invoices verifying authenticity. Clear, cold evidence accelerates removal.

8.3. Escalation to Legal

If Amazon stalls, escalate with an IP infringement complaint through Notice-Dispute email. Include USPTO registration certificate, design patent PDF, original proof. Mark subject "Urgent – Counterfeit Endangering Customer Safety." Lawyers speak decisive language; mirror it.

8.4. Customs Recordation

File your trademark and design patent with U.S. Customs and Border Protection. When shipments arrive bearing your mark from unknown shippers, CBP can detain and destroy. Overseas, use EU Customs Enforcement or China GAC IPR system. Odysseus blocked Trojan resupply lines by burning ships; you burn counterfeits at port.

---

9. Shield Maintenance — Audits and Varnish

Ajax polishes his shield before every march. You, too, must audit your defenses quarterly.

- **Trademark Renewal Calendar**: 5-year Section 8, 9-year Section 9 filings. Automate reminders.

- **Design Patent Fees**: pay maintenance at 3.5, 7.5, 11.5 years.

- **Brand Registry Health**: review new algorithm alerts daily; respond within 72 hours to preserve score.

- **Packaging Update**: as product line evolves, ensure every SKU still carries trademark.

- **Factory Oversight**: yearly unannounced audit to confirm molds are secured, scrap logged, overrun destroyed.

A shield neglected grows weak at rivets; a brand neglected soon belongs to the scavengers.

---

10. Action Checklist

- **Trademark**: run knockout search, file standard word mark in core class, store serial number.

- **Design Patent**: sketch novelty, file provisional, calendar conversion date.

- **Brand Registry**: enroll immediately with serial number, upload product images.

- **IP Accelerator**: if launch is <90 days away, engage for rapid filing.

- **Transparency**: request enrollment; integrate code printing into packaging artwork.

- **Project Zero**: submit five accurate infringement cases to qualify, then activate self-service deletions.

- **Compliance Vault**: compile lab reports, declarations, SDS; upload in Manage Compliance per SKU.

- **Off-Platform Patrol**: schedule monthly searches; file VeRO and DMCA where needed.

- **Cease and Desist Template**: prepare boilerplate letter; keep in quick-access drive.

- **Customs Recordation**: submit CBP online IPR application once trademark registers.

- **Quarterly Shield Audit**: review renewals, brand health alerts, packaging, and factory compliance.

---

11. Closing Formation

Homer's verse rings: "As long as each man's shield met the next, spears broke like reed stalks upon that iron hedge." Your goal is the same unbroken hedge: legal filings interlocked with Amazon programs, compliance dovetailed with patrol routines, every document ready to flash like bronze in the sun.

A brand that stands alone invites the fatal arrow. A brand in phalanx marches forward, driving pirates and price-gougers backward until they vanish over the horizon. Raise your shield now—file, enroll, serialize, patrol—and when the next counterfeit wave crashes, let it find only polished bronze and the unyielding glare of a company that knows the oldest lesson of war: **defense first, glory after**.

Chapter 5 – Hector's Resilience — Supply-Chain Endurance

1. Iliad Lens: Why Hector Matters to Logistics

When Achilles' war cry splits the air, most Trojans recoil. Hector alone steadies them. Homer gives us the portrait of a man who knows collapse is coming yet refuses to collapse himself. At the city gate, Andromache begs him not to return to battle. He answers, "*I have learned to be brave and to fight always among the foremost Trojans, upholding my great father's glory and my own.*" Later he concedes the odds: "*I know in my heart and in my soul that the day will come when sacred Troy shall perish.*" Still he pulls the helm over his head and steps back into the dust.

That mixture of realism and grit is the template for supply-chain endurance. You can read every macro-forecast—fuel spikes, currency swings, canal blockages—and still choose to march. But you do not march blind. Hector anchors Troy by preparing for what will fail: he drills backup battalions, ferries women and children inside the walls, studies Greek movements nightly from the ramparts. Resilient sellers do the same. Dual suppliers stand ready like relief squadrons; buffer stock fills the granaries; third-party logistics partners act as hidden gates through which fresh provisions flow even when the main gate is aflame.

The coming pages translate Hector's mindset into operational muscle. We'll hammer out dual-sourcing tactics, walk the math of safety inventory, weigh 3PL selection, and script a crisis playbook that absorbs port shutdowns, tariff shocks, and the lingering aftershocks of pandemics. By the end, you will not merely *hope* your supply chain holds—you will know where it bends, where it breaks, and where another shield already waits to plug the gap.

---

2. Dual-Sourcing — Two Helmets, One Head

2.1. The Philosophy: Never Fight Alone

Hector is never alone for long. When he charges, *"glorious Sarpedon went with him, and their army followed like a wall of fire."* The line teaches the core principle of dual-sourcing: a champion's power multiplies when a second champion shadows him. For you, that means no single factory, no single material vendor, no single packaging printer. One unexpected lockdown in Shenzhen, one chemical plant explosion in Gujarat, and your bestseller becomes a back-order apology.

2.2. Mapping the Critical Path

Begin by diagramming every component that touches your finished product: raw material, sub-assembly, colorant, packaging, instruction insert. Label each node with three attributes:

- **Switch-Time** — days required to relocate the step.

- **CAPEX Lock** — tooling or mold cost that would be re-spent.

- **Quality Variance Risk** — likelihood a new source changes specs.

Any node scoring "high" in two of three must gain a second supplier. That is your "Achilles strike zone"—if it fails, Greek spears reach the gates.

2.3. Qualifying a Second Supplier

Hector studies Greek tactics before meeting them. Likewise, you qualify a backup by mirroring every vetting step used on your primary:

- *Audit* — factory walk-through, video or in-person.

- *Sample* — golden sample run plus stress testing.

- *Compliance* — same certificates as primary or pathway to obtain.

- *Costing* — landed cost within 8 percent of primary; higher is acceptable only if risk offset justifies.

Do **not** treat the second supplier as a benchwarmer. Place at least 20 percent of volume with them immediately. Homer writes that Hector *"drove his horses through the ranks, testing every man."* You test suppliers in peacetime so they can perform in war.

2.4. Split or Parallel BOM

If your product uses specialized components—custom valve, printed circuit board—consider parallel bills of materials. Example for the collapsible bottle: valve A sourced from Korea, valve B from Malaysia. Both interface with the same neck threads. You keep two versions of finished goods SKUs but market them under one parent. Should one valve plant falter, you shift ad budget and variations toward the surviving child ASIN.

---

3. Buffer Stock Math — Filling the Trojan Granaries

3.1. First Principles

In Book XV, when Hector drives the Achaeans back to their ships, Homer notes, *"Troy was full of goodly stores within her walls, for the Trojans fetched what they needed day by day."* They had surplus, therefore flexibility. The modern version is safety inventory—units stored beyond forecasted demand to guard against supply disruptions and demand surges.

3.2. Service-Level Target

Select a service level—the probability of not going out of stock during lead time. Market leaders in competitive niches shoot for 95 percent; razor-thin margins may accept 90 percent. Convert the percentage to a Z-score (e.g., 1.64 for 95 percent).

3.3. Key Variables

- **Demand Mean (D)** — average daily units sold.

- **Demand Standard Deviation (σ_d)** — day-to-day fluctuation.

- **Lead-Time Mean (L)** — days from purchase order to fulfillment center checked-in.

- **Lead-Time Standard Deviation (σ_l)** — days of variance (port delays, customs holds).

3.4. Safety Stock Formula

$$\text{Safety Stock} = Z \times \sqrt{(L \times \sigma_d^2) + (D^2 \times \sigma_l^2)}$$

Work the numbers monthly. If volatility spikes—pandemic border rules, carrier strike—update σ_l and watch the safety stock floor rise like walls thickened overnight.

3.5. Buffer Location Split

Hector stations reserves in the inner city, not all at the walls. You mimic that by splitting buffers:

- **Origin Buffer** — 10–15 days of stock in factory warehouse; cheap storage, quick to load when PO spikes.

- **In-Transit Buffer** — 5–7 days on water or rail beyond plan, booked as "flex containers."

- **Destination Buffer** — 20–25 days in Amazon FCs or domestic 3PLs.

Divide to prevent simultaneous wipe-out by one failure point.

---

4. 3PL Selection — Choosing Allies Outside the Walls

When Hector wheels his chariot, he relies on charioteer Cebriones—skill and trust packaged in muscle. A third-party logistics provider is your Cebriones: invisible to shoppers yet crucial in maneuvering inventory.

4.1. Core Evaluation Axes

1. **Node Coverage** — ports served, proximity to major Amazon FCs.

2. **Turnaround Speed** — receiving time, prep time, outbound lead to FBA.

3. **Cost Transparency** — line-item quoting without bundled black boxes.

4. **Technology** — API or EDI integration with your inventory management.

5. **Damage Rate** — audit their claims per thousand units handled.

4.2. Stress Interview Questions

- "Describe your protocol when a container arrives flagged for FDA examination."

- "How many SKUs does your current largest Amazon client manage through you?"

- "Show last month's inbound appointments to ONT8; average wait?"

- "Hand me your escalation tree—names, phone numbers, after-hours contacts."

Their answers reveal whether their hoplites will hold shield line under midnight assault.

4.3. Contract Kill Clauses

Negotiate:

- **Storage Cap** — maximum pallets before overage; escalate cost bands clearly.

- **SLA Penalties** — credit for missing prep or ship windows.

- **Data Ownership** — your right to raw scan data.

- **Exit Timeline** — 30-day termination with 14-day release of all inventory.

Hector fought knowing Troy might fall; you must switch 3PLs without chaos if one fails.

---

5. Crisis Playbook — Helmets for the Firestorm

The night before Achilles returns, Hector tells his troops, *"Hold fast beside the beaked ships though the whole night through. We have no harbor but our hands and hearts."* Crises reveal who planned harbors. Below is a modular playbook you trigger on event thresholds.

5.1. Port Congestion or Closure

Trigger: Port dwell time forecast exceeds five days above average.

1. **Expedite Decision Matrix**

   - Divide inbound POs into A (bestsellers), B (steady sellers), C (slow).

- For A, shift from ocean to air or trans-load to alternate port; accept margin hit.

2. **FC Re-Route**

   - Use Amazon's inbound placement service to divert to east-coast FCs if LA/Long Beach jam.

3. **Listing Guard**

   - Reduce PPC on low-margin keywords to dampen velocity; comment on detail page "Temporary limited stock due to port delays—restock ETA posted here." Honesty buys patience.

5.2. Tariff Spike or Trade War

Trigger: New tariff schedule announced or duties jump >5 percent.

1. **Cost Shock Model**

   - Run landed cost delta; if margin under threshold, raise price gradually 2 percent per week while adding bundle value (bonus filter, pouch).

2. **Country Diversification**

   - Activate second supplier in duty-exempt country; shift molds or license designs under contract.

3. **Political Lobby Channels**

   - File for tariff exclusion if product meets niche humanitarian or environmental criteria. Hector sought alliances; you seek regulatory reprieve.

5.3. Pandemic or Health Crisis

Trigger: Factory lockdown, sudden freight capacity dip, or demand spike beyond 2× forecast.

1. **Health Documentation**

   - Secure "Safe to Work" certificates to avoid entire shipment rejection.

2. **Remote QC**

   - Install third-party inspectors with live video feeds; discourage forced closures by showing oversight.

3. **Demand Triage**

   - Prioritize SKUs with highest margin × turnover; temporarily delist low-margin variants to preserve cash.

4. **Customer Messaging**

   - Update product description top line: "We extended processing times by 48 hours to sanitize warehouses for staff safety." Transparency builds loyalty.

5.4. Currency Volatility

Trigger: Exchange rate moves 5 percent against you in 30 days.

1. **Forward Contracts** or **hedge** 50–70 percent of next quarter's payments.

2. **Supplier Share-the-Pain** clause—agree to split adverse movement beyond set band.

5.5. Data Breach / Cyber Attack on Logistics Partner

Trigger: Public disclosure or direct notice.

1. **Credential Reset** for all EDI/API tokens.

2. **Manual Switch** to redundant 3PL while forensic audit runs.

3. **Notify Amazon** through Account Health to pre-empt authenticity warnings if ASN feeds falter.

Each scenario sits in a binder (digital or paper), pre-filled with contact lists, templated emails, and financial models. When crisis strikes, you obey the book—emotion later, execution now.

6. Action Checklist

- **Critical Path Map** — list every component; label switch-time, CAPEX, quality risk.

- **Second-Supplier Onboarding** — audit, sample, compliance; shift 20 percent volume.

- **Parallel BOM** — design interchangeable components where feasible.

- **Service Level Set** — choose 95 percent or target; compute Z-score.

- **Safety Stock Calc** — plug D, σ_d, L, σ_l; update monthly.

- **Buffer Placement** — commit percentages to origin, in-transit, destination.

- **3PL Vetting** — score node coverage, speed, cost, tech, damage; run stress interview.

- **Contracts Signed** — storage caps, SLA penalties, exit terms.

- **Port Playbook** — write expedite matrix, FC reroute protocol, listing message draft.

- **Tariff Playbook** — cost model template, price stair, supplier shift plan.

- **Pandemic Playbook** — QC video protocol, demand triage, sanitation statement.

- **Currency Guard** — open forward contract facility, add FX clause to PO.

- **Cyber Shield** — token reset SOP, backup EDI partner.

- **Quarterly War-Game** — simulate one crisis per quarter; run table-top with team; debrief.

- **Resilience Journal** — after each disruption, log timeline, decision, outcome, lesson; refine playbooks.

---

7. Closing Stand on the Scæan Gate

Near the epic's climax, Hector faces Achilles outside the Scæan Gate. He tries to steady his breath, but *terror took hold of him, and he could not stay where he was but fled in panic.* Yet three times he circles the wall, finding courage at last to turn. That is the paradox of resilience: fear will come; what matters is the structure that lets you turn anyway.

Your supply chain will feel Achilles' shadow—trade rows, viral waves, ships wedged in canals. But each dual source, each buffer, each 3PL pact, each pre-written crisis drill is a circuit of the wall, buying you time to pivot and face the charge on ground of your choosing.

Where lesser brands flee until they drop, you will pivot, spear leveled, operations intact. And whether the day ends in victory or retreat, you will have another warehouse of stock, another supplier on standby, another plan sealed like bronze rivets along a shield rim. That is Hector's gift: not immunity from fate, but readiness to meet it on his feet. Go now—walk your line, count your arrows, call your allies—before the next sunrise over the dusty plain.

Chapter 6 – Agamemnon's Command — Numbers & Profit

1. Iliad Lens: The High King and the Price of Spoils

When the Greek kings divide their early plunder, Agamemnon stands, iron-shod sceptre in hand, and declares, "I am the greatest of the Achaeans, and therefore the fairest portion is mine." His words ignite Achilles' fury and, with it, the poem's central conflict. The passage is usually read as a lesson in ego; it is equally a lesson in **allocation**. Agamemnon sees first the gold he believes sustains authority, not the morale cost of seizing it. Homer's narrator warns, "Thus he drew to himself the wrath that would lay a thousand warriors in the dust."

The parallel for Amazon sellers is stark. Numbers drive every order—cost of goods, freight, fees, ad spend—yet if you chase raw revenue while starving margin, you will pull Achilles-level rage from cash flow itself. Whole lines of products keel over because the owner prized top-line trophies more than bottom-line oxygen. This chapter reclaims Agamemnon's sceptre and refits it with discipline: a complete unit-economics model, a landed-cost calculator, dynamic pricing rules that flex without panic, and a profit-first cadence that feeds war chests before vanity.

2. Unit Economics — Counting Spears Before the Charge

2.1. Why the Spear Count Matters

Ajax might swing a single giant pike, but the phalanx behind him must know exactly how many spears remain in the racks. Unit economics asks one unforgiving question: **What does one unit really earn after every hidden claw of cost has taken its bite?** You cannot answer with dashboards alone; you must carve the numbers like tally marks on a shield.

2.2. Complete Cost Stack

Write every component in long form—nothing hidden, nothing rounded.

- Raw material

- Labor or assembly charge

- Packaging inner, packaging master, inserts

- Mold amortization (divide by total planned units)

- Quality-control inspection fees

- Inland freight to port

- Export clearance and documentation

- Ocean or air freight

- Port drayage, customs duties, brokerage

- Domestic haulage to FBA or 3PL

- FBA inbound charge and label fees

- Amazon referral fee

- FBA pick-and-pack fee

- FBA storage (average dwell × per-cubic-foot rate)

- Advertising spend attributable per unit (campaign TACoS × selling price)

- Returns write-off percentage

- Warranty expense, if relevant

- Platform program fees—currency conversion, placement, remote fulfilment

Add them line by line. The moment you say, "Surely that one is negligible," remember Agamemnon brushing off Achilles' anger as negligible—an error that nearly loses the war.

2.3. Contribution Margin and Breakeven ACOS

When you have net cost per unit, subtract it from anticipated selling price to reach **contribution margin**. That figure then sets the ceiling for advertising cost of sale (ACOS). Formula:

Breakeven ACOS = (Contribution Margin ÷ Selling Price) × 100

If contribution margin is $9 on a $30 bottle, breakeven ACOS is 30 percent. Spend more and you bleed; spend less and you build surplus. Agamemnon kept no such check; when the plague struck, he spent prestige until morale bankrupted him. You will do the opposite.

---

3. The Landed-Cost Calculator — From Coast to Kill-Zone

3.1. The Voyage of the Crate

Homer follows a single shipment of spoils in Book I: "They placed the fair-cheeked girl upon the deck, they hoisted mast and sail, and the dark-prowed ship cut foam until it reached the wide roadstead of Chryse." Your goods take a modern but equally perilous journey. Every leg alters cost. Build a calculator—spreadsheet or purpose app—that lets you test scenarios in minutes.

3.2. Essential Inputs

- **EXW Price** – at factory gate.

- **FOB Add-On** – inland haul to port, documentation.

- **Freight Quote** – $/CBM or $/kg. Break this into base rate and surcharges: bunker, peak-season, Panama-Canal.

- **Insurance** – use 0.35 percent of cargo value unless specific.

- **Duty Rate** – HTS code × cargo value.

- **Port Fees** – terminal handling, chassis, demurrage buffer (average by port).

- **Domestic Leg** – rail or truck to 3PL/FBA, plus fuel surcharge.

- **Per-Carton Prep** – labels, polybag, bagging labor.

- **Inbound Placement Fee** – if you choose Amazon's "send to one FC" option.

3.3. Sensitivity Columns

Next to each input, build a +10 percent and −10 percent column. One blocked canal can add 15 percent to spot freight; a currency swing can shave 7 percent. The calculator shows whether margin still survives. Agamemnon never ran sensitivities; he bet everything on fixed tribute flows. When the gods cut them, his treasury trembled and he took Briseis to compensate, compounding loss with hubris.

3.4. Batch vs. Continuous Ordering

Freight and duty scale non-linearly. Run the calculator for 1,000 units, 3,000, 5,000. Sometimes doubling the order raises parcel storage but cuts per-unit transit cost by 40 percent. Sometimes the inverse is true when peak fees bite. The tool reveals which size loads the quiver with cheapest arrows.

---

4. Dynamic Pricing Rules — Adjusting Tribute Without Revolt

4.1. The Agamemnon Mistake

When Agamemnon's prestige shrinks, he grabs Briseis publicly. That single rigid act triggers a cascade he cannot reverse; no sliding scale, no compromise. Your price changes must behave opposite: **flexible, evidence-driven, invisible to the tribe**.

4.2. Demand Bands and Margin Floors

Define three demand signal bands per SKU:

- *High Velocity* — sales velocity >20 percent above 30-day mean.

- *Stable* — within ±20 percent.

- *Anemic* — >20 percent below.

Next assign margin floors (post-ads) aligned with inventory cover:

- If stock cover ≤30 days and velocity high, raise price by 3 percent until velocity returns to mean.

- If cover ≥90 days and velocity anemic, drop price by up to 5 percent, but never below margin floor set by unit economics.

Prices shift like tide, not earthquake. Use automated repricers (Amazon Automate Pricing or third-party) but gate them with guardrails so the algorithm cannot undercut margin floor. Achilles refuses to fight for free; neither should your listing.

4.3. Psychological Thresholds

Humans perceive 99 → 95 as a bargain but 95 → 93 as negligible. Adjust in sensible ticks: $29.95, $27.95, not $27.47. Record every move. Were the Trojans tracking the Greek camp's rations, they might have predicted supply shortages. You track price shift against sessions, conversion rate, ad cost, and organic position so tomorrow you can predict fate with sharper clarity.

5. Profit-First Cash-Flow Cadence — Filling the War Chest First

5.1. The Feast That Starved an Army

In Book II Agamemnon slaughters oxen for a lavish feast before dawn assault, then begs Achilles later for aid because the army's morale tanks. Lavish display without reserve drains power. The **Profit First** method (popularised by Mike Michalowicz) flips the order: slice profit first, run the kingdom on the remainder. For Amazon operations the cadence translates into weekly allocation sweeps.

5.2. Four Buckets, One Rhythm

- **Profit** — 10 percent of gross payouts wired to a sacred account; touch only for owner draws or reinvestment in new products.

- **Tax** — 15 percent; remit quarterly, never borrow.

- **Operating Expenses (OPEX)** — 35 percent; covers software, payroll, 3PL, misc fees.

- **Inventory + Ads** — 40 percent; purchase orders, freight, PPC.

Shift percentages by growth stage but keep profit non-zero. Seeing a dedicated profit account swell changes mindset: you become the high king funding victory, not the debtor begging gods for mercy.

5.3. Sweep Ritual

Every Friday, log into Seller Central, download the disbursement balance, transfer funds into buckets. Ten minutes. Ritual matters—like morning muster in the Greek camp where each soldier heard commands aloud. Habit brings clarity; clarity kills panic.

5.4. Buffer Reserve

When Friday sweep shows profit slice surpassing two months of payroll, divert extra into a **Resilience Fund** to absorb freight shocks, tariff hikes, legal fees. Hector saved grain for siege; your fund buys time to pivot when cost curves spike.

---

6. The Numbers War Room — Practical Implementation

6.1. Dashboard Hierarchy

1. **Daily** — SKU velocity, inventory cover, TACoS, breakeven ACOS flag.

2. **Weekly** — price elasticity notes, ad impression share, profit bucket sweep.

3. **Monthly** — landed-cost audit, sensitivity refresh, contribution margin for every SKU, 3PL invoice reconciliation.

4. **Quarterly** — FX impact, tariff review, freight contract renegotiation, kill or scale decision for each product.

Keep each view a separate sheet or BI card; mixing horizons breeds confusion. Odysseus plans night raids without mentioning decade-long return voyage; timeframes must stay pure.

6.2. Team Roles

- **Operations Analyst** — owns landed-cost calculator, updates inputs.

- **Pricing Strategist** — monitors demand bands, enacts price moves.

- **Finance Controller** — conducts profit sweep, tracks bucket balances.

- **Owner/General** — reviews numbers weekly, decides capital deployment.

Document. If a chariot driver falls, another grabs reins.

7. Action Checklist

- Build full unit-economics sheet; include every fee, every return.

- Calculate contribution margin and breakeven ACOS for each SKU.

- Draft landed-cost calculator with ±10 percent bands; test three order sizes.

- Choose service-level margin floor; encode guardrails into repricer.

- Define demand bands: high, stable, anemic. Write price moves for each.

- Open four bank accounts (profit, tax, OPEX, inventory+ads).

- Schedule Friday profit-first sweep; block calendar repeat.

- Establish resilience fund trigger—two months' fixed expense.

- Create dashboard views per time horizon; assign owner to each.

- Wargame one price-shock scenario and one duty-hike scenario; record responses.

- Review numbers with team every Monday; adjust tactics, not goals.

---

8. Closing Counsel

Late in the epic, when Hector is dead and Achilles drags the body, Agamemnon still thinks in silver talents and captured women. Yet he obeys when Achilles calls for funeral games; the high king finally honours structure over plunder. The message for you is simple: the throne rests on arithmetic, not aura.

You have forged the sceptre—unit economics precise as sword balance, landed-cost steel-nerved against storms, pricing rules that bend but never snap, profit buckets that fill before they spill. Hold that sceptre with the humility Agamemnon lacked, and your empire of ASINs will not depend on luck or sacrificial pleas to distant gods. It will depend on numbers you can recite like Homeric verse, rhythm steady as drumbeat oars driving a long ship toward new horizons.

Chapter 7 – Patroclus' Push — Launch & Early Reviews

1. Iliad Lens: Borrowed Armor, Borrowed Time

Patroclus never intended to eclipse Achilles. His single aim was to shove the Trojans back from the ships before the kindling caught. The plan was audacious yet limited: wear Achilles' armor, strike hard, buy breathing room. Homer writes, "He leapt into the battle like a god, and the Trojans, when they saw the gleam of Peleus' son, were shaken, for they thought the swift-footed one himself had come." Panic alone broke the front.

That scene is the perfect allegory for Amazon's honeymoon period, the brief stretch—roughly the first thirty days after an ASIN's first confirmed sale—when the algorithm treats your brand-new listing as if it already wore Achilles' bronze. You gain priority indexing, accelerated relevance testing, and conversion weighting that would otherwise take months to earn. Yet the armor is borrowed. The minute Patroclus lingers, Hector notices subtle tells, calls the bluff, and kills him. Likewise, if your listing dawdles, if reviews lag, if conversion underperforms, the algorithm withdraws its provisional favor and ranking slides.

Patroclus' charge therefore becomes our blueprint:

- **Speed:** A surge so decisive that competitors cannot counter-adjust during the window.

- **Deception-through-familiarity:** Presenting signals—photo quality, A+ polish, social proof—that mimic established heroes.

- **Purpose:** Not to win the whole war but to establish beach-head rankings long enough for real brand momentum to arrive.

Hold that image: a hero in borrowed gear sprinting straight for the point where flame licks hull. Your launch sequence must move with the same urgency and clarity.

---

2. The Honeymoon Ranking Period — Hour-by-Hour Timeline

Amazon does not publish the rules, but data across thousands of launches paints a reliable map. Picture the next section as Patroclus' mad dash drawn in sand—each milestone a footprint between the wall and the ships. Adjust for product life cycle, but keep the cadence.

Day -30 to -7: "Camp Council"

- **Inventory in Place:** At least two months of forecasted sales already checked in. Stock-outs during honeymoon are fatal.

- **Offer Prepared:** Title, bullets, images, A+ content, brand story—all live, not placeholders.

- **Price Anchored:** Premium if you hold a clear USP; otherwise at or slightly below market average.

- **Keyword Trench Map Finalized:** Core ten exact-match phrases, twenty mid-volume variants, fifty long-tails. Manual campaigns built but paused.

Patroclus walks the rows of Myrmidons, checking spearheads. You test every link: listing loads fast, mobile renders correctly, parent-child variation set works.

Day -6 to -1: "Armor Donning"

- **Helium 10 Index Check:** Confirm index for all target keywords. If any fail, tweak phrase placement; wait twelve hours; re-index.

- **Search-Find-Buy Seed Orders:** Five to ten authentic buyers execute guided searches on unique long-tails, find your listing organic, purchase at full price. Spread over three days. This conditions the algorithm to see relevance before official launch.

- **Ad Pre-heat:** Start AUTO campaign at token $5/day purely to gather data; bids low enough not to spike sales yet.

Day 0: "Gate Crash"

The minute FC shows "received," trigger:

- **Manual Exact-Match Blitz** on ten long-tails at top-of-search placement, high bid, daily cap equal to ten units each.

- **External Burst:** Send 30–50 visitors from an owned email list or micro-influencer story swipe-ups. Tag links through Amazon Attribution. Purpose: session diversity.

- **First 20 Units** priced with five-percent coupon to push conversion above category median.

Like Patroclus swinging Achilles' spear, you are signalling to the algorithm, *I belong on page one.*

Day 1–3: "Shock Wave"

- **Review Pipeline Opens.** Use Request-a-Review button for every order ninety minutes after carrier shows delivered.

- **PPC Expansion:** Turn on broad-match campaigns; keep budget discipline but allow algorithm exploration.

- **Price Holds.** Resist temptation to slash further; early conversion data trains ranking model.

Day 4–7: "First Heroic Deeds"

- **Amazon Vine Enrollment:** If brand-registered and under 30 reviews, enroll twenty-five units. Vine Voices equal Homeric bards; their detailed feedback lends gravitas.

- **Post-Purchase Email #1:** TOS-compliant thank-you (no incentives, no review ask). Content offers PDF quick-start guide or tips.

- **Influencer Unboxings:** Ship three micro-creators (10–50k followers) product with no script. Their organic stories widen social proof.

Day 8–14: "Momentum or Stall?"

Check metrics:

- **Session Volume:** Should trend upward 20–30 percent over first week.

- **Unit Session Percentage:** Aim above category median (usually 12–15%).

- **Review Count:** Target 10–15 organic+Vine reviews by Day 14; star rating ≥ 4.5.

- **Organic Rank:** For at least three core long-tails, crack top 25.

If any lag, adjust:

- **Increase Budget** on winning campaigns.

- **Audit Listing Copy** for weak persuasion; refine bullets.

- **Consider 10-percent Coupon** on low-rank phrases to
  spike conversion.

Day 15–21: "Holding the Line"

- **Auto Campaign Negative Harvest:** Add non-converting
  terms as negatives; raise bids on converting search terms.

- **External Traffic Wave 2:** Short press-release or niche
  blog feature.

- **First Insert-Driven Reviews Arrive:** More on inserts
  below.

Day 22–30: "Handing Armor Back"

Patroclus' window closes; algorithm resets ranking weight to
normal. Goals:

- **Anchor Organic Position** for five long-tails in top ten, two
  mid-volume terms in top 20.

- **Reach 25–30 Reviews,** average ≥4.5.

- **Stabilize TACoS** below 25 percent (or your breakeven target).

- **Begin Price Normalization** if you launched at promo; raise in 2-percent increments every 72 hours while watching conversion lag.

When Achilles finally dons fresh armor, momentum continues—the product now fights on its own merits, not honeymoon grace.

---

3. Early Reviewer Programs — Voices in the First Chorus

3.1. Vine as Modern Rhapsode

In Homeric times, professional poets called rhapsodes spread heroic tales. Amazon's Vine Voices function similarly. They receive product free, disclose the fact, and publish extensive, often image-rich reviews that the algorithm treats as high authority. Key tactics:

- **Submit Highest-Differentiation Variant First.** Unique color or bundle ensures Vine Voice photos stand out among copycat listings.

- **Prepare Unboxing Experience.** Voices critique packaging; sloppy presentation invites a three-star nuance that will linger.

- **Include Quick-Start Insert** with concise instructions to minimize early user error—patents may protect design, but nothing shields you from a misfired first impression.

Vine slots fill quickly; enroll Day 4 latest to ensure reviews land during honeymoon.

3.2. Post-Purchase Email Sequence

Amazon allows two emails: shipment confirmation (system generated) and one seller-initiated message per order. Best practice:

- **Timing:** 24 hours after delivery confirmation to ensure item has been experienced.

- **Tone:** Gratitude, brevity, no marketing fluff.

- **Content:** Link to troubleshooting video on YouTube (unbranded landing, no sales funnels).

- **Review Ask:** Use "Request a Review" button in Seller Central instead of phrasing request yourself, keeping risk near zero.

Patroclus never begs fame; his deeds speak. Your product must likewise earn, then lightly remind.

3.3. Inserts That Pass TOS

Amazon policy forbids inserts offering gifts for reviews or steering star rating. But it allows genuine customer service resources. Craft an insert that obeys three golden lines:

1. **Serve First:** Front side thanks customer, includes QR to PDF manual, warranty registration that **does not condition benefits on reviews**.

2. **Brand Story Brevity:** Twenty-word origin line: "Born on alpine trails, built to keep families light." Emotional spark; no ask.

3. **Support Path:** Email and SMS helpline for issues. On the reverse, a single sentence: "If we earned five stars today, share your experience on Amazon; if not, we will fix it." That phrasing, approved by precedent, does not explicitly solicit positive bias nor offer compensation.

Inserts arrive the moment customer opens box—like Patroclus' first trumpet blast. If they build confidence, reviews flow organically.

3.4. External Reviewer Pods (Whitehat Only)

Communities on Facebook, Discord, or niche forums allow honest, rebate-free product seeding. Conditions:

- **Disclosure:** Recipients must state "I received this product free for testing" when posting off-Amazon.

- **No Review Gate:** They may or may not review on Amazon; you neither require nor track.

- **Objective Content:** Encourage high-resolution photos and real-world use.

While such content does not always convert directly to Amazon reviews, it fuels social proof loops that lift conversion, therefore ranking.

---

4. Inserts, Inserts, Inserts — Spearshafts of Persuasion

4.1. The Psychology

A customer tearing bubble wrap resembles a warrior unsealing loot. Dopamine spikes, rational filters dim: perfect moment to cement emotional narrative. Achilles' shield dazzled friend and enemy alike upon first sight. Your insert should astonish by clarity and relevance.

4.2. Design Anatomy

- **Size:** 4 × 6 inches postcard, heavy matte stock.

- **Front Visual:** Full-bleed lifestyle photo, product in use, evocative but uncluttered.

- **Headline:** Seven words max, active verb first: "Pack Light. Move Farther. Stay Dry."

- **Sub-header:** One-sentence brand mission.

- **QR Panel:** Bottom left; icon plus text "Scan for quickest setup & tips."

- **Support Icons:** Email, SMS, social handle. No more than three.

4.3. The Warranty Gambit

Amazon forbids conditioning warranty on review. Offer unconditional 18-month coverage. Then, in follow-up email after warranty registration, invite feedback through "Request a Review." By decoupling benefit from review, you obey TOS and still route satisfied customers toward public praise.

4.4. Quality Loop

Each quarter, sample 100 returned units, read the reason codes, update insert FAQ and QR-linked manual accordingly. Patroclus rode out wearing borrowed armor; you must mend dents fast before Achilles sees them.

5. Beyond A-to-Z: Handling Early Negatives

A single one-star in week one echoes Hector's spear through Patroclus' belly. Countermeasures:

- **Lightning Response:** Under two hours for public comments; apologize, offer immediate refund or replacement.

- **Root-Cause Dive:** Is issue related to materials, instructions, FBA mishandling? Fix process within 48 hours.

- **Follow-Up:** Once customer accepts solution, gently ask if satisfaction now matches expectations; some volunteers remove or revise review.

Do not file removal requests unless review violates policy (hate speech, obscene, competitor sabotage). Authentic negatives mixed with majority positives prove trustworthiness.

---

6. Action Checklist

- **Inventory Prepared:** Two months' supply received before Day -7.

- **Listing Locked:** Complete copy, images, A+ live Day -7.

- **Keyword Seed Orders:** Five to ten search-find-buys executed over three days pre-launch.

- **Day 0 Blitz:** Exact-match manual campaign, external traffic burst, limited coupon active.

- **Review System:** Request-a-Review automation toggled; first ask ninety minutes post-delivery.

- **Vine Enrollment:** Submit twenty-five units by Day 4.

- **Insert Finalized:** TOS-compliant postcard printed, packed in all inventory.

- **Post-Purchase Thank-You:** Single email sequence live.

- **Metric Targets:** 10–15 reviews, 4.5-star average, top-25 rank on three long-tails by Day 14.

- **Adjustment Loop:** Check sessions, conversion, TACoS daily; tweak bids, copy, coupon as needed.

- **Negative Review SOP:** Two-hour reply, 48-hour root-cause fix.

- **Quarterly Insert Update:** Incorporate top three customer confusions into new revision.

7. Closing Flame on the Horizon

Patroclus fell, but the ground he seized mattered. The Greek ships no longer smoked; the Trojans, rattled, drew back to regroup. His push bought Achilles the motive to re-enter war and, ultimately, to decide the siege. Your launch aims for the same strategic lever. Thirty days of manic focus, of sleepless monitoring, of ethical persuasion will win you a foothold that compounds: more reviews invite more purchases which earn more rank which draw more profit.

Remember the price Patroclus paid for hesitation. When he chased glory beyond the plan, Apollo struck him dazed and Hector delivered the blade. Do not overreach. Exit the honeymoon by Week 4 with stock stable, ads profitable, and social proof humming; then step back, analyze, and let the machine run at measured cadence.

Chapter 8 – The Embassy — Negotiation Mastery

---

1. Iliad Lens: When Words Must Move Mountains

Night has fallen over the Greek camp. Hector's firebrands flicker against the black, and the surf pounds like a slow war-drum. Inside Achilles' hut the air is tense with harp strings and private grief. Agamemnon, stripped of options, sends his finest talkers to fetch the only warrior who can save the ships. Odysseus, Phoenix, and Ajax cross the sand together: three modes of persuasion, three facets of a single skill every seller must master—negotiation.

Odysseus speaks first, framing the stakes with sober logic:

> "Son of Peleus, the Greeks are in dire straits.
> Round every trench the Trojan fires are burning.
> If you hold back, tomorrow we shall haul our ships to sea."

He offers quantified incentive—"seven tripods, ten talents of gold"—and positions himself as agent, not rival. The speech is reason tethered to tangible benefit.

Phoenix follows with memory and emotion:

> "Such, dear boy, was the counsel of your father that
> day
> he sent you forth from Phthia.
> 'Win word-fame,' he said, 'but curb great pride.'
> I have been a father to you; hear me now."

He does not barter; he **reminds** Achilles who he is. This is
identity-based persuasion.

Ajax, last, takes the stance of collective shame:

> "Let us be gone, for all our words are spoken in vain,
> and yet the heart within you is pitiless.
> The gifts offered are noble; the men who beg you are
> your peers.
> Think on the horror, and bow to your own."

He leverages peer status and face—powerful forces in any
culture.

The embassy fails because Achilles' anger is still volcanic, but
Homer shows every lever a negotiator can pull: logic and reward,
story and belonging, status and loss of honor. Bring those levers
to the factory floor, the freight forwarder's office, or the piercing
realm of Seller Support, and you walk in legendary footsteps.

---

2. Principles Distilled from the Embassy

1. **Multi-Voice Strategy**
   Send more than one negotiator when the stakes justify it,
   each carrying a different style—numbers, narrative, peer

solidarity. One message seldom moves all hearts.

2. **Sequence Matters**
   Odysseus goes first because reason clears ground for emotion. Phoenix follows because shared history softens the will. Ajax finishes with a blunt mirror of consequences. Order your own arguments: factual anchor → emotional bridge → social proof.

3. **Offer Must Outweigh Ego Cost**
   Agamemnon's gifts look rich, yet Achilles sees them as ransom for lost honor. Your supplier or Amazon rep also weighs unspoken costs (face, workload, KPIs). Package gains so they eclipse those hidden losses.

4. **Leave With Dignity Intact**
   The embassy departs without threats. Tomorrow they must fight beside Achilles if he returns. Never scorch a relationship you may need at dawn.

---

3. Supplier Negotiation Scripts — Bronze Tongues in the Boardroom

3.1. Opening Inquiry: First Arrow Loosed

Subject: New Project RFQ – Collapsible Silicone Bottle (Projected 50 K Units / Year)

Hello [Factory Name] Team,

I am [Your Name], brand owner of Palm-Fold Gear in the United States.
 We will launch a new collapsible water-bottle line this quarter and seek a manufacturing partner for a minimum of 50,000 units across three colorways in the first year.

What we need today

1. EXW quotation for 5,000-unit pilot run

2. Material certifications (FDA 21 CFR 177.2600; LFGB)

3. Photos of similar products you have produced

4. Standard tooling cost and lead time

We will shortlist two suppliers for in-person audit next month. Timely, detailed answers will secure priority.

Kind regards,
 [Signature]

Why it works — concise BLUF, clear quantities, compliance ask up front. You anchor volume but hold final figure for leverage.

3.2. Price Counter: Shield Edge to Shield Edge

Supplier: "Our price is USD $2.85 / unit EXW for 5,000 pcs."

You: "Thank you. At $2.85 we cannot reach target landed cost. Based on our calculator, we need $2.40 for the pilot to be viable.

What options could close that gap—material tier, packaging adjustments, or sliding scale on future orders?"

You invite collaboration, not ultimatum. Offer three levers so the supplier can save margin elsewhere.

3.3. Concession Bundle: Gifts for Achilles

After back-and-forth you push:

"Let's summarize:
 • Unit price $2.55 for pilot 5,000 pcs
 • Tooling $1,800 amortized over first two orders
 • Payment 30 % deposit / 70 % against inspection pass
 • Exclusive design protection with $10,000 penalty for third-party production
 If we hit 10,000 pcs monthly by Month 4, you raise price to $2.60 to cover capacity ramp. Does this structure work?"

You concede a future price rise (supplier honor) in exchange for immediate savings (your honor). Mirror Agamemnon's chest of gold, but attach conditions that secure your campaign.

3.4. Lead-Time Compression Script

"Current quote shows 45-day production. Our launch window demands ship date in 32 days. We can split order: 2,000 pcs air-freight at our cost if you finish those in 25 days. Remaining 3,000 by sea on original schedule. We will pay 50 % deposit today to fund overtime. Confirm feasibility by tomorrow, please."

Here you shoulder part of burden (air cost) to make request credible. Achilles respected bravery; suppliers respect shared pain.

3.5. Quality Dispute Diplomacy

If inspection fails:

"We received QIMA report indicating 18 % units with lid-seal failures above 3 psi. Our AQL stipulates 1.5 %. Please propose corrective action within 24 hours. Options we see:
 • Full re-inspection after 100 % manual test (your cost)
 • Immediate rework of faulty batch plus $0.10 / unit credit on entire order
 • Cancel PO with deposit refund

We value long collaboration and prefer option one if you have staffing."

Offer doors; let them choose dignity.

---

4. Amazon Support Escalation Tiers — Climbing the Palace Steps

Negotiating with Amazon is unlike factory talk; it is closer to Odysseus navigating layered courts of kings.

Tier 0: Self-Service Redress

Before opening any case, recreate issue in a test environment.
Screenshot error messages, ASIN stats, and violation notices.
Many wrongs die here.

Tier 1: Seller-Support Frontline

Case template:

Subject: ASIN B09XYZ — Incorrect HazMat Flag Removal
Request
 Body (BLUF first):
 "Please remove the HazMat flag applied on 7 July 2025. The
product is FDA-grade silicone, non-pressurized, and exempt under
UN classification 0000. Supporting documents attached: SDS, lab
test, prior Amazon hazmat approval ID #12345678."

Then bullets: timeline, impact, ask. End with polite sign-off and
contact hours.

Frontline reps work scripts. Provide every checkbox for them.

Tier 2: Captive Account Support / SAS Core

If Tier 1 loops or answers inaccurately, open case and in first line
write: "Escalate to Captive Team." Attach previous
correspondence. Captive reps have systems access to override
flags.

Tier 3: Executive Seller Relations ("Jeff Team")

Craft a one-page narrative:

Opening sentence: "I am requesting Executive Intervention because repeated support cases have failed to resolve a safety flag that threatens customer choice and brand integrity."

Paragraph 2: facts and chronology.
Paragraph 3: resolution requested.
Paragraph 4: risk to Amazon customers if ignored.
Attach PDF to jeff@amazon.com. Use sparingly; think Achilles in armor—once unsheathed, must strike true.

Tier 4: Notice-Dispute / Legal

For IP or defamation issues unresolved, send formal notice to Amazon Legal with evidence bundle, CC outside counsel. Be factual; courts may read it.

---

5. Advanced Tactics — The Odyssean Toolbox

1. **Information Asymmetry Mining**
   Before quoting, pull Chinese export data (Panjiva, ImportGenius) to see what volume factory already ships at what price. Knowledge tames exaggeration.

2. **Silence Countdown**
   After stating counter-offer, count to ten quietly. Humans hate vacuum; let the other side fill it with concessions.

3. **Anchored Framing**
   Present high "ideal" package first (bronze-armor level),

then work down to "realistic" (plain helm). The concession
feels bigger.

4. **Flinch & Pause**
    When supplier names price, audible intake of breath plus
    pause shows misalignment without hostility. They often
    self-edit.

5. **Conditional Yes**
    Agree on point contingent upon another: "Yes, we can
    stretch payment terms to 45 days **if** you guarantee
    exclusive mold custody."

6. **Written Confirmation**
    End every call with email: "Thank you for today's
    discussion; my notes state…" Phoenix reminds Achilles of
    childhood stories—memory seals deals.

---

6. Action Checklist

– Study the embassy speeches; label logic, emotion, status
elements.
  – Draft RFQ email using BLUF; send to five suppliers.
  – Prepare cost target sheet before price talk.
  – Build concession bundle matrix: what you can give (lead time,
batch size) vs. must gain (price, exclusivity).
  – Script silence countdown into calls; practice with colleague.
  – Set Amazon case template; store docs (SDS, certificates) in
cloud for instant attach.

- Map escalation ladder; log case IDs chronologically.
- Create one-page executive escalation format; file blank copy for emergencies.
- Schedule quarterly supplier review—price, quality, capacity.
- Document every agreement in writing within 12 hours.

---

7. Closing Voice — Words Sharper than Bronze

Odysseus could not cool Achilles' wrath, yet his speech buys the Greeks one more night; Phoenix plants doubt; Ajax plants shame. Negotiation is rarely single-stroke victory—it is cumulative pressure applied with craft. When you win a ten-cent price drop, gate a counterfeit takedown in one email, or secure reimbursement after six denied cases, remember the beach at dusk: three men walking back through dim fires, no triumph yet, but the war still winnable because they dared to speak.

Homer ends the scene with the embassy's silent march across the sand, torches guttering. Your own return paths will feel the same—tired eyes, pages of notes, numbers spinning. Carry them proudly. Tomorrow's battles are easier when tonight's words were clear, honorable, and unrelenting.

Chapter 9 – Zeus-Level Vision — Data & Ads

1. Iliad Lens: The God Who Sees the Whole Plain

When Hera and Athena plot against Troy, Zeus sits on Ida and surveys both armies "as one who weighs in golden scales the fates of men, tilting life and death with a finger." He sees every spear flash, every prayer whispered into a shield rim, every puff of dust that marks a chariot wheel. The thunder-lord does not guess; he **knows**. Knowledge is domination.

Your advertising strategy must rise to that cloud-height. While competitors scrap over keyword bids like foot soldiers slugging in mud, you hover above them with a panoramic dashboard—real-time TACoS curves, session rates, glance-view tides, brand-share storms rolling in from social. Zeus-level vision means ❶ collecting every relevant data spark, ❷ wiring those sparks into one coherent lightning bolt, and ❸ striking precisely the hilltop that tips the whole battle.

We will forge three weapons in this chapter:

- **PPC Campaign Architecture** that obeys the grammar of search, display, and brand placements.

- **Signal Rivers**—how clicks, costs, and conversions flow together into the core metrics: TACoS, session percentage, glance views, new-to-brand share.

- **Dashboard Forging** followed by an **Action Cadence**—because even a god must hurl the thunder at set moments or clouds drift by unused.

Hold in mind Zeus' warning to lesser divinities: "Sit apart and watch, nor dare to bend the balance." He allows no meddling guesswork. Either your data truly rules your ads, or you delude yourself and fall like doltish Ares, wounded and whining.

---

2. PPC Campaign Architecture — Forging the Lightning Rods

2.1. Core Philosophy

Amazon advertising is not one battlefield but three concentric rings:

1. **Search** — the hand-to-hand press where Sponsored Products rule.

2. **Display** — flanking maneuvers launched through Sponsored Display or DSP.

3. **Brand / Video** — banners atop scroll, trailers mid-search, the heralds proclaiming lineage.

Zeus throws different bolts for earth, sky, and sea; you must craft unique campaign families rather than one sloppy mega-campaign.

2.2. Sponsored Products – The Phalanx

- **Structure:** Build one exact-match campaign per hero SKU for each high-intent keyword cluster. Name convention: "SP-EXACT-[SKU]-[KW-ROOT]".

- **Budget:** Assign separate daily caps so a runaway star cannot drain the army's entire grain store.

- **Bid Strategy:** Start at 50 % above suggested top-of-search bid for first seven days, then inverse-taper: if placement conversion < product average, throttle by 10 % increments every 48 hours.

Next, create **broad-match discovery campaigns**. Funnel data: every broad search term with 1+ sale moves to a **phrase-match intermediate**, and from there to exact once it proves two sales at < breakeven ACOS.

This ladder mirrors Greek ranks: raw recruits in the reserves, seasoned hoplites forward, heroes in the vanguard.

2.3. Sponsored Brands – The Heralds

Sponsored Brands lift your crest above the dust like Achilles'
plume flashing "like Sirius rising." Craft headline with star-word
first ("Fold-Proof Bottles"), then proof snippet ("100% Leak-Free"),
then soft CTA.

- **Placement:** Top-of-search only for launch month; loosen to
  rest-of-search once CTR surpasses 0.7 %.

- **Brand Store Link:** Land clicks on sub-page devoted to the
  product family, not generic home page. Show them the
  palace, not the whole city.

Include **Video** sub-type at Day 14, once reviews pass twenty-five.
Video auto-plays; even mute footage of bottle collapsing and
springing erect loops in the mind like an epic simile.

2.4. Sponsored Display – The Flank Riders

Display targets two prey:

- **Product Targeting** — raid competitor pages; set ROAS
  goal 2:1 minimum.

- **Audiences** — remarket to views without purchase last
  fourteen days; bid up 20 % during seasonal peak.

Cap frequency to 2 per day per shopper. Zeus' thunder only needs
to rumble twice before awe sets in; past that, lightning fatigue.

2.5. DSP – The Siege Engines (Optional)

Once monthly revenue tops $200 k, lease Amazon DSP to retarget off-site. Segment by **lifestyle** (outdoor parents) plus **in-market** categories (hydration gear). Keep initial CPM bids low; tune creative every two weeks.

Just as Greeks hauled stone throwers only after foot troops secured the beach, bring DSP once core Sponsored Products already profit.

---

3. Signal Rivers — Reading the Weather on Ida

3.1. TACoS – Total Advertising Cost of Sales

TACoS = Total Ad Spend ÷ Total Revenue. Unlike ACOS (ad-revenue only), TACoS measures true gravity. A falling TACoS while revenue climbs means ads push organic tail. A rising TACoS signals you borrow growth on credit.

Target:

- **Launch Month:** up to 35 % acceptable.

- **Stabilize Month 3:** drive under 20 %.

- **Mature:** 10–12 % as moat.

3.2. Session Percentage

Unit Session Percentage = Units Sold ÷ Sessions. Think of sessions as mortals raising eyes to Olympus; units as those who sacrifice. 15 % is baseline in most soft-goods niches; 20 % is hero-grade. Ads can raise sessions but only listing power lifts percentage.

3.3. Glance Views

Glance views are page-loads recorded when shoppers hover product tiles or land on listing. Sponsored Display and DSP feed them silently; spikes here foreshadow future session surges. Track ratio:

Glance-View-to-Session Ratio. If it swells, ads spraying awareness are working; if sessions lag, thumbnails intrigue but listing fails to convert.

3.4. New-to-Brand % (for SB and SD)

Zeus counts worshippers; you count fresh shoppers. Aim for 70 % new-to-brand in first quarter of advertising; retreat to 40 % once installed base thickens.

3.5. Share of Voice

Manual scrapes or tools show percentage of top-of-search slots you hold on tracked keywords. Every 10 % share delivers compounding organic rank lift. Zeus does not merely cast thunder; he occupies sky.

4. Dashboard Forging — Building the Oracle

4.1. Tool Stack

- **Databricks or BigQuery** pipeline connecting Amazon Advertising API, Selling-Partner API.

- **Power BI, Looker, or Tableau** as visualization layer.

- **Scheduled ETL** every four hours for high-velocity SKUs.

4.2. Must-Show Tiles

- Daily TACoS heatbar (seven-day rolling)

- ACOS per campaign family

- Session % trended against price moves

- Glance views versus sessions

- Keyword share of voice heatmap

- Inventory cover overlay (so you never stoke demand past stock)

Each tile links drill-through to SKU view, down to single keyword. No scroll labyrinth; Zeus' throne room is uncluttered marble.

4.3. Alerts & Automation

- **Slack alert** if TACoS rises >5 % day-over-day.

- **Email digest** of keywords whose ACOS swings past breakeven by 10 %.

- **Bid automation** that lowers bids 15 % on terms with ACOS 20 % above target for three days straight.

- **Budget re-allocation** script: pushes 10 % budget from campaigns with ACOS < target ÷ 2 to those within target ± 5 % but limited by impression share.

Divinity lies in never sleeping. Your scripts are Argus-eyed watchmen.

---

5. Tactical Cadence — The Thunder Cycle

Day-to-day toil means nothing without pattern. Zeus governs seasons; you govern spend.

- **Daily Dawn Review (15 min)** — TACoS tile, inventory cover, budget left. Adjust bids ±5 % max to avoid knee-jerk chaos.

- **Mid-Week Deep Dive (45 min)** — Explore search-term report; graduate performing terms; negate bleed.

- **Friday Cross-Ring Sync (30 min)** — Compare brand ads new-to-brand % with Sponsored Product conversions. Decide whether to fuel top-funnel weekend.

- **Month-End High Council (2 hrs)** — Bring finance, ops, creative. Show dashboard trends; realign goals: "We will drop TACoS by two points while holding revenue; raise session % by one point via new video." Assign tasks.

This cadence matches lunar cycle of Trojan campfires Homer lists—phases of flare and lull, all under one deity's gaze.

---

6. Creative Iteration — Sharpening the Bolt

Amazon auto-transcodes, dims, and loops. Win within those rules.

- **Thumbnail Refresh** every sixty days on Sponsored Brands—change background hue or tagline.

- **Video Hook** first three seconds: product solving pain, no talking heads.

- **Display Banner** 80 % image, 20 % text; largest legible font; negative space like a storm gap.

- **Copy Rhythm** mirrors epic meter: powerful verb / tangible benefit / emotional aftertaste.
  Example: "Fold, Clip, Run — Water minus weight."

Measure CTR deltas; retire the weak.

---

7. External Data Wind — Forecasting Storms

Zeus hears prayers; you hear whispers:

- **Google Trends** for core keywords; spike? preload budgets.

- **Weather data** (heat wave drives hydration gear).

- **TikTok mentions** via scraper—when content virals, allocate defensive bids to brand terms to catch spillover.

Predict, don't react.

---

8. Action Checklist

- Map three-ring campaign structure; launch exact, phrase, broad ladders.

- Set initial bids 50 % above suggested, taper by data.

- Spin Sponsored Brand headline: verb + proof + CTA.

- Produce 15-sec loop video; deploy Day 14.

- Track TACoS daily; alert at +5 % swing.

- Build dashboard with tiles: TACoS, session %, glance views, SOV.

- Initialize automation rules for bids, budgets, alerts.

- Schedule daily, weekly, monthly review cadence.

- Refresh creatives on 60-day timer.

- Harvest external signals—Google Trends, weather, TikTok—to pre-shift bids.

---

9. Closing Thunderclap

In the climactic Book VIII, Zeus lifts his golden scales: "Heavy with fate, the day of doom sank for the Achaeans; the Trojans' lot climbed high toward blazing heaven." With a tilt he changes destiny. Data and ads give you that scale. Misread the beams, and your product sinks like Ajax under Hector's boulders. Read them rightly, act in rhythm, wield lightning only where stone must shatter, and you command the weather itself.

Rise to the cloud-height, austere as the storm-king. Let competitors brawl in fog below while your dashboard horizon lights with every strike you choose. Numbers are thunder; timing is flash; vision is deity. And when morning sun reveals rankings rearranged, let it show your banners bright upon Ida, unrivalled under the vault of clicking sky.

Chapter 10 – Night Raid — Competitive Intelligence & Defense

1. Iliad Lens: When Darkness Turns to Advantage

Odysseus and Diomedes move through the enemy camp like thoughts through a dream. Homer shows them slipping past guard fires, slaying sentries, and stealing the Trojan spy Dolon's horses. The text pulses with the dread of men who know that night hides both predator and prey:

> "Silent as wolves that feast on flesh yet drip no blood upon their paws,
> so went the two through gloom, and none beheld them."

Daylight rules favor massed armies; night favors those who read shadows. Amazon never sleeps. Your competitors tinker with repricers at 2 a.m., hire black-hat services to vomit one-star reviews at dawn, or clone your listing with their own FBA inventory while you dream. If you rely on daylight vigilance alone, you will wake to burnt ships.

Night-raid strategy for the seller splits into two mandates: **(1) unblinking surveillance** and **(2) crisp retaliation scripts**. This chapter teaches the sensing networks—price-war monitors, review-attack radars, hijacker tripwires—and the counter-moves that fire within minutes, not days.

---

2. Shadow Watch: Monitoring Price Wars

Price is the torch spies carry. You see it flare on search results before you see banners, reviews, or storefronts. If mine drops by three dollars overnight, you know someone is probing your flank.

2.1. Baseline Grid

Begin by engraving a baseline: record your own retail, coupon, and strike-through price plus those of the top five competing ASINs at 09:00 local time for seven straight days. This log becomes your "peace price." Anything diverging more than 7 percent triggers investigation.

2.2. Automated Crawlers

Tools such as Keepa, Sellerise, or custom Python scrapers (if your tech stack allows) can ping product pages every hour and flag:

- price undercut ≥ 5 percent

- new coupon or promo stack

- sudden deletion of prior coupon (signal of inventory exhaustion)

Output to Slack channel #watch-tower. Zeus-level dashboards from Chapter 9 feed off these pings, so your view of the storm includes competitor flashes.

2.3. Interpreting the Flare

Not every drop is a war:

- **Clearance Move** — Price plummets, coupon stacked, inventory graph (Keepa) shows cliff. Ignore; they're liquidating.

- **Seasonal Tease** — Two-day flash coupon aligned with holiday. Prepare but do not match; stick to your own promo calendar.

- **Sustained Drip** — Five days straight, pennies at a time. That is trench warfare to erode Buy Box and rank. Act.

2.4. Counter-Fire Playbook

1. **Margin Audit**: Confirm your floor. If you can undercut without bleeding, schedule *match minus 1 percent* for 48 hours.

2. **Value Stack**: Rather than price cut, raise perceived value—add bundle coupon, free accessory, or extended warranty note. Trojans heard strange armor; fear grew.

3. **Ad Pressure Shift**: Pull budget from overlapping keywords; push to long-tail fortress keywords where your

differentiation shines.

4. **Support Messaging**: Quick banner on listing—"Price drop locked for 72 hours." Signals confidence.

Remember, Odysseus kills Dolon and takes intelligence, not prisoners. Act decisively; restore previous price once rival blinks.

---

3. Review Attacks: When Enemy Tongues Turn Daggers

Homer's night raid ends with the slaughter of sleeping Thracians, a strike that removes reinforcements before they stir. Modern black-hat sellers aim for your social proof while you sleep, waking you to a wall of one-star reviews referencing defects that don't exist.

3.1. Sentinel Metrics

- **Review Velocity Spike** — More than 3× your daily review average, positive or negative.

- **Keyword Cluster** — Same adjective ("cancerous," "toxic") appears in five new reviews.

- **Midnight Cluster** — Multiple reviews between 01:00 – 04:00 with no accompanying orders in that window.

3.2. Early-Warning System

- **ReviewMeta / Fakespot API** monitoring your own ASIN. If quality score drops 10 percent overnight, alarm.

- **Brand Dashboard** automated review notifications via email; forward to Slack.

- **Manual Glance** — Every morning, read top three "Most recent." Discipline: five minutes.

3.3. Triage Protocol

1. **Screenshot & Archive** each suspect review URL, rating, timestamp, and profile.

2. **Cross-Check Orders**: In Seller Central, run "Manage Orders" filter by buyer name if provided; absence hints fake.

3. **Policy Violation Report**: Use "Report abuse" link under review for content that includes hate, profanity, competitor mention, medical claim. Keep phrasing "This review violates Amazon Community Guidelines section X."

4. **Customer-Service Comment**: Public reply within two hours: express regret, state surprise, offer immediate replacement/refund. Outside readers see your professionalism; algorithm notes responsiveness.

3.4. Wider Counter-Spy Net

- **Reverse Profile**—click attacker's username; if they reviewed unrelated products with the same wording, capture screenshots; include in escalation.

- **Escalate** to Community-help@amazon.com with compiled evidence and case IDs. Subject: "Pattern Review Abuse – ASIN B09XYZ – Urgent."

- **Legal Letter** if defamation damages brand (e.g., "causes cancer"). Real attorneys plus documented loss often prompt faster removal.

As Diomedes takes a chariot team after slaying Rhesus, convert attack into asset. Offer the chariot: publish blog post detailing your lab test results, linking to Amazon listing. Doubters become believers.

---

4. Hijacker Tripwires: Guarding the Gates

When Trojans hide within Troy's walls, they become undifferentiated; conversely, when a stranger sells under your ASIN, shoppers can't tell from thumbnail who packs the box. That counterfeit or gray-market seller leeches Buy Box, tanks price, invites negative reviews for defects you didn't create.

4.1. Detection Lattice

- **Brand Registry automated alerts**: Enable "Potential Infringers" emails.

- **Sellerboard or Helium 10 Alerts**: Monitors number of offers per ASIN; ping Slack when >1.

- **Manual Search**: Weekly query "buy used & new."

4.2. First-Strike Email

"Hello [Seller],

You are listing ASIN B09XYZ under brand-registered trademark Palm-Fold. We do not recognize your supply channel.
 Please reply within 24 hours with purchase invoice or we will file infringement reports per Amazon policy."

Tone calm, not hostile. Many hijackers are arbitrage novices; they retreat.

4.3. Brand Registry Report

If no response: open Brand Registry > Report a violation > Trademark. Attach:

- Trademark reg certificate

- Photos of product with branding

- Screenshot of offending offer

Amazon often removes in 48 hours.

4.4. Last Resort — Test Buy & Legal

Order item, record unboxing video, capture differences (no logo, inferior packaging). File A-to-Z claim citing counterfeit; attach video to support ticket. Escalate to Notice-Dispute if unresolved.

As Odysseus strips slain Dolon of wolf-skin cloak to prove mission, you must keep physical evidence of counterfeit for any future courtroom.

---

5. Counter-Moves: CS-Alert Macros & Automated Defenses

5.1. CS-Alert Macros

Create canned responses within Seller Central's "Messaging":

- **"Defect Alarm – Replacement & Data Request"**
  Apologize → ship replacement same day → ask for batch code photo.

- **"Gray-Market Warning"**
  Identify unauthorized seller; instruct customer to inspect packaging for missing hologram; offer free return and

official unit.

Macros reduce response time under one hour. Amazon tracks seller response speed; early replies protect account health.

5.2. Automated Alerts

- **FBA Inventory Pulse**—Set threshold (e.g., 30 days cover). If hits, ad budgets auto-throttle to prevent forced price wars.

- **Repricer Guardrail**—Stop repricing below margin floor. Hijackers often spark downward spiral; your iron limit preserves ROI.

- **Review Keyword Watch**—Zapier flow: when new review contains "counterfeit," push urgent Slack ping.

5.3. "Night-Widow" Cron Jobs

Run after midnight UTC:

- Scrape top-20 competitors for coupon changes.

- Compare their star rating delta; if they climb, study new tactics next morning.

- Log screenshots to S3 bucket for historical trend.

Bloodless spies update your war map while you sleep.

---

6. Psychological Defense: Preventive Narratives

Achilles' shield not only blocks blows; its myth deters attack. Embed deterrence in listing:

- **Brand Story Module**: Show factory line inspecting anti-counterfeit holograms.

- **FAQ**: "Is this sold by Palm-Fold only?" Answer clarifies authenticity checks.

- **Insert Card**: Holographic sticker with serial; instruct buyer to confirm via site. Hijacker sales drop when customers return units flagged unauthentic.

Perception of impregnable gates discourages casual siege.

---

7. Action Checklist

- **Baseline Price Log** for you and five rivals (7-day run).

- **Set Keepa/Sellerise price alarms** at ±5 percent variance.

- **Install Slack channel #watch-tower** with review, price, hijack integrations.

- **Draft CS macros** for defect, gray-market, counterfeit scenarios.

- **Enable Brand Registry automated protections**; verify trademark attached to all SKUs.

- **Weekly manual review scan** of last 10 reviews per ASIN.

- **Set nightly cron scrape for competitor coupons & ratings**.

- **Prepare infringement evidence folder** (trademark cert, design patent, packing photos).

- **Design anti-counterfeit insert** with hologram & serial verification URL.

- **Practice test-buy protocol**—assign team member quarterly to order your own ASIN from Buy Box and confirm authenticity chain.

---

8. Closing Torch in the Dark

The night raid ends with Odysseus driving stolen horses back to Greek lines while the first red clouds of dawn appear. He grins, not from bloodlust but from knowledge gained. The severed head of

Dolon is grisly, yet it is intelligence embodied: proof that Troy's watch can be pierced.

Your ecommerce night raiding is less bloody but equally vital. You will not see the algorithm's eyes widen at 3 a.m., but you will feel its verdict by morning—rank preserved, rating steady, price equilibrium intact. Or not, if you slept without sentries.

Keep the watchfires low, the scripts ready, and the shadows full of your own unseen scouts. Then, when light returns, let rivals blink in disbelief at a fortress stronger than before, wonders greater than sleep could conjure. In Homer's tongue: "Thus they rejoiced who came unscathed back over the plain, their hearts bold, their knowledge richer, while the enemy woke to cries of loss."

Chapter 11 – The Ransom of Hector — Customer Service That Calms Rage

1. Iliad Lens: The Night Two Kings Share Bread

Achilles has dragged Hector's corpse round and round the barrow of Patroclus. Day after day the Trojans watch their champion bruise against the dust. Then, one cold night, an old man in plain cloak walks unarmed into the strongest hut on earth. Priam kneels and kisses the hands that killed his son.

> "Remember your own father, Achilles, and pity me."

Homer lets silence swell. From the darkness of the hut comes the sound of the swift-footed killer sobbing. Moments later, Achilles lifts the king gently. He calls for clean water to wash the body, orders food, and swears an oath of safe passage. Enemy and avenger eat at one table. Rage melts because empathy speaks the only language sharp enough to pierce armor.

Everything Amazon calls "customer service" is a lesser echo of that scene. Somewhere out in the ether a shopper feels wronged. If you ignore them, they drag your star rating behind their chariot until it crumbles. If you lean forward—kneel, metaphorically, at the edge of their pain—you can do what Priam did: ransom the

relationship for a cost smaller than the havoc it would have
wrought.

---

2. The Inner Logic of Complaint

2.1. Rage Is a Claim on Dignity

Shoppers rarely rant because of dollars lost. They rant because
identity feels threatened. A leaking bottle mid-trail says, "You are
unprepared." A mis-shipped size tells a parent, "You failed your
child's birthday." Your first goal is not correction but restoration of
dignity. Priam does not lead with gold; he leads with shared
mortality: "Think of your own father."

2.2. Time Multiplies Emotion

Homer keeps the timing precise: Priam steals in the same night
Hector's body was last dragged. He bridges sorrow before it
calcifies into hate. Modern corollary: the longer a ticket sits, the
higher the refund cost and the louder the review. Response-time
SLA is therefore strategic, not clerical.

2.3. Reparations Must Feel Symbolic

Achilles grants not merely the body but a twelve-day truce. That
concession is far larger than Priam's ransom weight in gold.
Over-deliver. If policy allows a replacement, upgrade shipping to
overnight. If refunding, include 10 % coupon toward next
purchase. Money is metric; gesture is solace.

3. Architecture of a Priam-Grade Service System

1. **Channels:** Amazon messaging, email from insert card, social DMs, phone fallback.

2. **SLA Targets:** Replies in < 2 h between 7 a.m.–11 p.m. local; < 8 h overnight.

3. **Knowledge Base:** Live index of FAQs, replacement process, warranty rules, refund math.

4. **Empathy Protocol:** Greeting, mirror emotion, responsibility acceptance, resolution path, gratitude.

5. **After-Care Loop:** Follow-up within seven days; request updated sentiment or review revision.

Build structure first so agents can act like kings, not scribes fumbling scrolls.

4. Message Templates — Words That Unbend Spears

4.1. "Faulty Product" — Immediate Replacement

Subject: We'll Make This Right Today

Hello [Name],

I'm devastated to hear your Palm-Fold bottle leaked on the trail. I use ours on weekend runs with my own daughter, and I know how fast a small leak can ruin an outing.

I've already ordered a new bottle for overnight delivery—no charge, no return needed. I'll email tracking a bit later this evening. If you prefer a full refund instead, just hit reply and I'll process it within minutes.

Thank you for giving us a chance to fix this. We build these bottles so parents can adventure lighter, never heavier.

Warm regards,
[Agent]
Customer Care, Palm-Fold

4.2. "Late Delivery" — Shipping Carrier Error

Subject: Your Package Fell Behind — I'm Catching It Up

Hi [Name],

I see the carrier scan paused in Louisville for over 24 hours. That is unacceptable. I've filed an urgent ticket with UPS and in parallel set a replacement to ship Amazon Prime Next-Day. If the original box eventually arrives, feel free to donate it to a friend or local outdoor club—our treat.

Thanks for your patience. I'll update you tomorrow whether UPS finds the first parcel.

—[Agent]

4.3. "One-Star Public Review" — Outreach via Comment

"[Customer], this is Jack, founder of Palm-Fold. I just read your review about the hinge failure. Please accept my sincere apologies. Could you email me at help@palm-fold.com? I want to send a free replacement designed with our newer steel-pin hinge and also dissect what went wrong so we can prevent repeats."

The public sees accountability. Many reviewers update to four or five stars once resolution lands.

4.4. "Abusive Language" — Boundary Yet Grace

"Hello [Name], I understand you're frustrated and I want to solve this quickly. I'm committed to respectful dialogue so we can get you a working bottle or full refund. Could we keep language clean while we sort this out together?"

Never mirror aggression. Achilles' calm after Priam's plea is your compass.

5. Refund Math — Gold Measured Against Wrath

5.1. Cost of Letting Anger Fester

A single one-star can knock conversion five percent for months. If SKU sells 30 units/day at $30 with 20 % margin, that five-percent dip costs about $900/month contribution. Spending $15 overnight shipping to hush rage is trivial.

5.2. Replacement Threshold Formula

Replace if:

```
(Replacement COGS + Shipping) < (Expected lost
margin from negative sentiment × probability of
review staying)
```

Because probability hard to measure, heuristics: if claim within 45 days and tone polite → replace by default. If obvious misuse and rude → offer half-price code or instruct on proper use.

5.3. Warranty Budget Line

Allocate 2 % of monthly revenue to "Hector Ransom Fund." Track payouts. If fund drains early, investigate manufacturing. If surplus stays > 3 months, consider lengthening warranty to differentiate brand.

6. Turning Returns into Loyalty

6.1. "White-Glove Refund"

When refunding, include digital thank-you card explaining design evolution. Offer early-access seat for product-testing circle. People who see the workshop join the cause.

6.2. "Second-Chance Insert"

Every replacement ships with small card: "We fixed the problem you experienced. If this new bottle isn't perfect, text my direct line." Signed by founder. Converts victims to evangelists.

6.3. Story-Share Funnel

Ask happy replacement recipients for adventure photos. Feature them on social; tag them. Heroification cements loyalty stronger than discount codes. Priam leaves Achilles' hut praising him to every courtier; same echo modernized.

---

7. Operational Rituals

1. **Daily Stand-Down (09:00)** — scan overnight tickets; escalate chronic defects to ops.

2. **Evening Gratitude Sweep (20:00)** — send follow-ups for tickets resolved 48 h earlier.

3. **Weekly Rage Report** — list top complaint themes, mean handle time, refund outlay, review delta.

4. **Monthly Empathy Drill** — agents role-play difficult customer, colleagues respond until solution delivered in < 5 minutes.

Rehearsal makes compassion fast. Priam rehearsed speeches before entering Achilles' hut; Homer notes him "pondering his words in the dark."

---

8. Handling Edge-Case Disasters

8.1. Injury Allegation

If user claims harm, immediate steps:

- ask if they need medical attention, offer to cover cost;

- collect details: circumstance, batch code, photos;

- cease speaking of liability, forward to product-safety lead;

- issue full refund + gear recall instructions.

8.2. Social-Media Firestorm

Within 30 minutes:

- acknowledge publicly, "We see the issue and are investigating,"

- DM aggrieved poster with cell number,

- pin statement on profile,

- launch landing page with running updates,

- coordinate with legal before admitting fault if facts unclear.

Speed and transparency quell mobs faster than polished excuses. Achilles returns Hector within hours, not days.

---

9. KPIs That Matter

- First-response time

- Resolution time

- Customer-touches per ticket

- Refund ratio versus order count

- Post-resolution review delta

- Repurchase rate of replacement recipients

Monitor weekly. Celebrate downward trends; drill rising ones.

---

10. Action Checklist

- Install helpdesk software with SLA timers (Zendesk, Freshdesk).

- Write four empathy templates; load into macros.

- Fund 2 % revenue "Ransom" refund budget.

- Print replacement insert signed by founder.

- Schedule daily and weekly service rituals.

- Build dashboard tracking KPIs above.

- Draft product-injury protocol, store with legal.

- Run monthly empathy drill.

- Share every week's Rage Report with product team for design fixes.

- After each resolved ticket, send follow-up within seven days.

---

11. Closing Breakfast in the War-Tent

Achilles hands Priam a loaf and cup:

> "Let us sit in quiet, King, and eat our grief away,
>   for iron hearts are fed on pain,
>   yet even sorrow yields to bread and wine."

Customer service is that bread and wine—the meal that turns wailing into weary gratitude. You cannot undo a leak, a delay, a cracked hinge. What you can do is kneel in the digital dust, call the buyer by name, reverse the humiliation, and send them out believing the brand on their receipt belongs to human beings of honor.

Do this and each anger answered becomes, paradoxically, another verse in your own heroic song, the song that tells new shoppers: **Here is a house where even enemies leave fed and comforted.**

Chapter 12 – Burning Troy — Scaling & Exit

1. Iliad Lens: The City in Flames and the Long View Beyond Victory

In the final cycle of Trojan agony, Homer lingers on fire. "Up to the roof-trees leapt the ravening flame, and all the city's cry rose on the wind." The Achaeans do not torch Troy for spite alone; they raze it so that no rival can rebuild from its embers. Yet the poem ends not with ash but with ships preparing to sail home, holds stuffed with ransom gold, captives, and bronze. The true prize is not the blaze—it is the wealth and reputation that blaze secures.

For an Amazon seller, "burning Troy" is the moment when market share peaks, competitors falter, and the brand stands poised to expand far beyond its original walls—or to cash out at premium and sail on. This chapter fuses two imperatives: **scaling without collapse** and **exiting without regret**. Both demand the same eagle-height view with which Achilles scans the fleeing Trojans: an ability to see farther than today's click and tomorrow's payout.

2. Multi-Channel Expansion — Planting Flags on New Shores

2.1. Why Leave the Beach at All?

When Hector dies, Troy's inner keep still stands. The Greeks light torches and race to breach new gates because static victory rots. In e-commerce, relying on one marketplace courts sudden policy shifts, fee hikes, algorithm updates. Diversify before crisis erupts, not after.

2.2. Direct-to-Consumer Storefront

Build a branded Shopify store that feels like the megaron of a king—spacious, story-rich, frictionless checkout. Route Instagram and TikTok traffic here first. Use Amazon Buy with Prime badge if eligible so conversion uplift piggybacks on Prime trust while data stays yours. Collect emails; segment; nurture. Think of DTC as the base camp from which you raid every other channel.

2.3. Big-Box Wholesale

Approach REI, Dick's, or Target once Amazon reviews exceed one thousand with 4.6-star average. Buyers respect proof. Present a sell-through deck: weekly velocity numbers, seasonality graph, and photo of palletized units in 3PL ready to drop-ship. Wholesale margins are thinner, but shelf presence amplifies brand prestige—"spoils" that impress acquirers.

2.4. International Marketplaces

Expand to Amazon Canada, UK, EU, then Japan and UAE. Quote from Homer rings here: "Wide as the range of earth and sea the gifts of the gods are scattered." Register trademarks abroad six months before launch; translate listings with native copywriters, not AI alone. Hire local VAT agent so tax compliance does not ambush you like Paris' arrow from the tower.

2.5. Social Commerce Integration

TikTok Shop and Meta Checkout convert impulse into instant cart. Clip fifteen-second collapse-demo loops from your Sponsored Brand video; overlay price plus Buy button. Keep SKUs limited—hero product only—to avoid inventory chaos on platforms still refining logistics.

2.6. Retail Bundles

Bundle collapsible bottle with clip, filter, and micro-fiber towel. New SKU, new UPC, same parent listing. Bundles lift AOV and discourage price trackers because comparing apples to apples fails when each apple now comes entwined with bespoke stem. Homer's Greeks load prize tripods, horses, and women into the same ship; the cargo mix multiplies value per voyage.

3. Brand Bundles & Collection Logic

3.1. Narrative Cohesion

Bundles must obey story logic. Achilles' armor pieces belong together because Hephaestus forged them as a set. Your hydration kit should echo one mission: "go farther, lighter, safer." Packaging inserts depict a trail scene using every item inside. Cohesion raises perceived worth more than sum of parts.

3.2. Price Laddering

Create three rungs: Solo, Duo, Expedition. Keep psychological gaps: \$29 → \$49 → \$79. The middle wins the most share; the high tier seeds aspiration.

3.3. Ops Simplicity

Kitting done at 3PL avoids China over-packing fees and lets you flex components based on seasonal demand (add insulated sleeve in winter). Track kit BOM in inventory software so shortages of towels don't hide behind parent SKU counts.

4. FBA vs. 3PL Mix — Logistics After the Sack

4.1. FBA Strengths

Prime badge, nationwide two-day network, multichannel fulfillment at low per-unit pick. During scaling, keep at least thirty days of high-velocity SKUs inside FBA to preserve search rank and Buy Box.

4.2. FBA Fragilities

Restock limits swing like Zeus' thunderbolts. During Q4 you may find yourself capped at half normal cubic feet. Removal fees spike; aged inventory fees burn. Therefore tether FBA to a domestic 3PL holding buffer stock equal to another thirty days.

4.3. 3PL Roles

- **Kitting & Bundling** — assemble kits on demand.

- **DTC Fulfillment** — Shopify and TikTok orders.

- **Retail Pallet Prep** — UCC-128 labels, ASN compliance.

- **Return Refurb** — inspect, sanitize, re-box.

4.4. Dynamic Allocation Rules

Algorithm inside your IMS checks daily velocity, Amazon restock limits, and 3PL on-hand. If FBA can receive, create inbound; if full, flip extra Amazon orders to Seller-Fulfilled Prime through 3PL. Zeus sees whole plain; your system must too.

---

5. Valuation Levers — Setting Troy's Ransom

When Achilles ransoms Hector, the weight of gold bowls over the scales. So too will your brand's asking price when acquirers arrive. Five levers tilt that balance:

1. **SDE or EBITDA Margin** — improve via COGS renegotiation and TACoS decline trend.

2. **Growth Rate** — demonstrate quarter-over-quarter climb, especially off-Amazon.

3. **SKU Concentration** — diversify revenue so no single ASIN > 30 % unless hero moat is impregnable.

4. **IP Strength** — trademarks, design patents, utility patent in prosecution.

5. **Operational Independence** — documented SOPs, outsourced logistics, minimal owner hours (< 10/wk).

Each full point of EBITDA margin can add 0.5× multiple. Each extra channel with > 10 % revenue share can add another 0.25×. Build levers early; valuation compounds like interest.

---

6. Due-Diligence Prep — Cleaning the Treasury

Priam does not count coins in Achilles' hut; he pre-weighs ransom before leaving Troy. Likewise, prep documents months ahead:

- **Financials** — monthly P&L and balance sheet three years back, by channel.

- **Tax Filings** — federal, state, VAT if international.

- **Supplier Contracts** — MOQs, price sheets, exclusivity clauses.

- **IP Dossier** — certificates, applications, cease-and-desist victories.

- **Ad Account Access** — share read-only token for proof of TACoS trend.

- **Customer Service SOPs** — templates from previous chapter.

- **Inventory Aging Report** — show slow movers addressed via discount cycles.

- **Legal** — no ongoing litigation; if any, summarize risk.

Store in cloud data room. Label folders logically: 01-Financial, 02-Ops, 03-IP… Due-diligence teams love neatness; it signals hidden costs unlikely.

---

7. Broker Checklist — Choosing Heralds to Speak for You

Odysseus negotiates ransom better than Menelaus because words are his craft. A broker sits in that Odyssean role.

- **Niche Expertise** — track record closing FBA-heavy CPG brands 5–20 M.

- **Buyer Network Depth** — strategic (Unilever), aggregators, PE funds.

- **Fee Structure** — 10 % on first million, 7 % next four, 5 % beyond. Retainers okay if credited back.

- **Valuation Philosophy** — uses trailing twelve months but adjusts for inventory and add-backs.

- **Marketing Package Quality** — teasers, CIM (Confidential Information Memorandum) with narrative flair.

- **Bidding Process** — sets deadlines, collects LOIs, guides to SPA.

- **Post-Close Support** — earn-out consulting clause to maximize contingent payouts.

Interview three; request sample CIM. Choose the one who asks hardest questions—they uncover skeletons before buyers do.

---

8. The Exit Dance — From LOI to Closing

1. **Letter of Intent** received with purchase price, structure (cash, seller note, earn-out), exclusivity window.

2. **Exclusivity Clock Starts** (usually 60 days). Provide documents within 48 hours; delays shrink trust.

3. **Quality of Earnings Audit** by third party. Answer every clarification within 24 hours.

4. **Purchase Agreement Draft** negotiates reps, warranties, indemnities.

5. **Inventory Count** cut-off date set; adjustment formula agreed.

6. **Transition Services Agreement** spells owner hours post-close.

7. **Closing and Wire**—funds hit, stock certificates transfer, brand registry ownership change, ad accounts re-permissioned.

Keep separate counsel experienced in e-commerce exits; Achilles carries his own shield, not Hector's.

---

9. Post-Exit Legacy: What Comes After the Smoke

Homer ends not with loot tally but with the burial of Hector and red dawn. Life continues. If you stay on as advisor, guard brand voice. If you walk away:

- Invest in new markets.

- Mentor founders.

- Write the next epic.

"The fire died, yet hope walked on," the poet might have said had he followed the fleet home.

---

10. Action Checklist

- Map new sales channels: Shopify, TikTok Shop, EU Amazon; set launch quarters.

- File trademarks in upcoming markets six months prior.

- Design three-tier bundle ladder; prototype at 3PL.

- Implement FBA-3PL auto-allocation logic in IMS.

- Negotiate COGS to lift EBITDA margin two points pre-sale.

- Document SOPs and reduce owner involvement below ten hours weekly.

- Build data room: financials, IP, contracts, tax, SOPs.

- Interview at least three brokers; secure one with niche success.

- Clean aged inventory; run discount cycle.

- Prepare trauma list—potential skeletons—to disclose early.

- Set personal post-exit plan: advisory retainer or clean break.

11. Final Ember

As night swallows the glow of burning Troy, a hush settles over the plain. The Greeks ship their spoils, but each man knows tomorrow will demand new seas, new storms, and fresh harbors. You reach scaling or exit not to rest but to voyage farther—armed with gold, yes, but richer still in the craft of conquest you have learned chapter by chapter. Keep the oars beat steady, the lookout high, and the memory of flame alive as warning: grow beyond the walls before someone else climbs them, sell before the fires dim, and always sail on while the wind of story fills your sail.

Conclusion & Next Steps — *Write Your Own Epic*

The Twelve Timeless Principles Re-Forged

1. **Scout the Walls before Sailing**
   Achilles' ankles flash only because the Achaeans first measured Troy's height. You, too, take no step without numbers.

2. **Sharpen One Unbeatable Edge**
   "Swift-footed Achilles" is remembered for speed, not for breadth. Your product's unique promise must cut the noise in a single stroke.

3. **Slip the Trojan Horse Past the Gate**
   Odysseus proves that story disarms suspicion. A listing infused with narrative enters where blunt discounts cannot.

4. **Interlock Shields**
   A hoplite phalanx never exposes a gap. Register the brand, patent the shape, serialize the units—let no arrow find soft timber.

5. **Stock Grain for the Siege**
   Hector's Troy endures ten years because storage rooms stay full. Dual sources, buffer stock, and 3PL allies keep

your line from breaking.

6. **Count the Spoils with Cold Eyes**
   Agamemnon's vanity costs lives. Unit economics, landed cost, and profit-first cash sweeps keep pride from bankrupting victory.

7. **Charge in Borrowed Armor, then Withdraw**
   Patroclus uses honeymoon glory, then hands the field to durable process. Launch hard, then settle into calibrated growth.

8. **Speak with Three Voices**
   Odysseus reasons, Phoenix remembers, Ajax shames. Negotiate suppliers, Amazon reps, and buyers with logic, story, and shared honor.

9. **See the Whole Plain**
   Zeus watches TACoS, session rate, glance views, share of voice—all at once. Let dashboards make you thunder-sighted.

10. **Move under Moonlight**
    Night raids monitor price cuts, review strikes, counterfeit incursions. Automations wake before dawn so you sip coffee instead of panic.

11. **Feed the Enemy and Win a Friend**
    Priam's humility melts rage. A refund given fast, a replacement overnighted, or a simple apology typed at midnight averts years of hatred.

12. **Burn the City, Save the Fleet**
    When domination arrives, scale to new channels or sell at
    terms of strength—leave nothing half-done for embers to
    re-ignite against you.

Carry these maxims like polished stones in a pouch. When the
algorithm shifts or a pandemic snarls docks, rub each one and
recall how a bronze-age line of verse already foretold the solution.

A Spoken-Aloud 90-Day War Plan

*Days 1-7 — **Recon & Rally***
 Stand on the dune and gaze. Gather keyword volume, competitor
prices, margin scenarios. Audit FBA limits and 3PL capacity.
Announce to the team the single number that will crown the
campaign—perhaps "break-even TACoS under twenty-one" or
"forty reviews at 4.7 stars."

*Days 8-21 — **First Sortie***
 Launch exact-match ads. Seed long-tail search-find-buy orders.
Enroll in Vine. Respond to every ticket inside two hours. Hold
stand-up calls daily; measure session percentage like pulse.

*Days 22-45 — **Fortify & Expand***
 Split inventory: half in FBA, half in 3PL. Turn on Sponsored Brand
video. Draft DTC site copy. Negotiate second molds. Initiate
monthly price-war scrape.

*Days 46-60 — **Night Raids & Diplomacy***
 Set automated review keyword alerts. Test-buy top competitor.

Re-quote freight for order two. File trademark in Europe. Pitch an Instagram micro-creator set for unboxing week.

*Days 61-75 — **Council of Captains***
 Read dashboards with finance, ops, creative. Trim ad bids where ACOS bleeds, double where ROAS dazzles. Update insert to answer newest complaint. Draft bundle packaging.

*Days 76-90 — **Torch & Triumph***
 Soft-open Shopify with Buy with Prime. Load first bundle kit at 3PL. Record three-minute founder story for TikTok Shop launch. If exit is the aim, prepare CIM outline and short-list brokers. Celebrate with six-hour offline retreat; plan next quarter's shore to storm.

Recite the plan out loud each dawn; a spoken objective steels the will better than silent sheets.

Glossary of Epic & Amazon Tongues

- **Achaean Algorithm** – the unseen ranking logic that decides whose spear hits the Buy Box.

- **Adroitness of Odysseus** – uncanny knack for turning limited budget into disproportionate clicks.

- **Bronze Boss** – the trademark at the center of a brand's defensive shield.

- **Crested Helm** – any highly differentiated hero image that signals quality before price.

- **Dolon Data** – intelligence captured by scraping a rival's keywords or stock levels.

- **Fires on Ida** – sudden fee increases or restock limits foreseen only by god-eye dashboards.

- **Golden Scales of Zeus** – the TACoS graph where profit and spend tilt hour by hour.

- **Myrmidon Cadence** – team ritual of short, fierce stand-ups followed by silent, efficient work.

- **Patroclus Window** – the thirty-day launch grace granted to new ASINs.

- **Phalanx Protocol** – layered IP, compliance, and detection programs locking shields.

- **Ransom Weight** – cash or gesture allocated to turn an angry customer into vocal fan.

- **Scæan Gate** – keyword threshold where page-one rank converts at double the scroll depth below.

- **Troy in Flames** – the moment your category share crosses thirty percent and expansion or exit beckons.

Speak these terms until they roll off the tongue; a shared dialect forges fast cohesion.

Further Reading & Resource Links

- *The Iliad* translated by Richmond Lattimore – study cadence and metaphor for copy inspiration.

- *Profit First* by Mike Michalowicz – rewire cash-flow instinct.

- *The Goal* by Eliyahu Goldratt – learn to view supply chain as critical path, not warehouse.

- *Never Split the Difference* by Chris Voss – modern Odysseus tactics.

- Brand-building spreadsheets, KPI dashboards, and SOP libraries live at **palm-fold.com/war-room**. Bookmark the page; each file updates as algorithms evolve.

Final Call to Arms: Iterate or Be Conquered

Achilles returns Hector's body yet swears to keep sharpening his spear. You must do likewise. The marketplace tomorrow is not the beach you landed on today. New fees, new voices, new arrows darken each sunrise. A product that ruled summer can die by winter if complacency takes the wall.

Therefore write your own epic each quarter. Scratch old victories from the shield and hammer fresh reliefs: new bundles, fresh channels, leaner costs, faster replies, kinder refunds, clearer dashboards. If you ever feel the flame of ambition dim, open Homer again, read the night Priam walked through tents of murderers and left with his son in his arms. Empathy won that impossible bargain. Discipline, numbers, and story will win yours.

Close this book, not to shelve it, but to let it ride at your side like a second blade. Sing your brand aloud. Stand on the virtual ramparts and watch the horizon for sails. They are always coming. With edge honed and heart awake, meet them in strength, and carve your name so deep that even the next burning city cannot erase the echo. Go, commander—the field awaits.

THIS IS NOT A COLLECTION

This volume is part of **Ancient Wisdom Hacks**—
an ongoing body of work focused on how strategy, power, and
failure actually function under pressure.

The books are only one layer.

What you are reading is an entry point into a larger system of
interpretation, application, and expansion.

WHAT THESE WORKS ARE DESIGNED TO DO

Most people look for answers.

These works expose patterns:

- How decisions are made before they are visible
- How systems weaken before they collapse
- How power shifts before it is recognized

This is not theory.
It is applied observation.

THE SYSTEM BEHIND THE WORK

Across all volumes and future releases, three forces remain
constant:

- **Strategy** — how outcomes are shaped before action
- **Conflict** — how people and systems break under pressure
- **Power** — how control is gained, maintained, and lost

No single book contains the full picture.
Each adds another angle.

CONTINUE BEYOND THIS VOLUME

New interpretations, applied volumes, and extended works are
released continuously.

To access current and future material, visit:

www.AncientWisdomHacks.com

WHAT YOU WILL FIND

- Additional applied volumes across industries
- Expanded interpretations of foundational texts
- New releases not available through standard distribution
- Future projects extending beyond books

The system is still expanding.

FINAL POSITION

Clarity does not make outcomes easier.

It removes the illusion that they were ever simple.

Ancient Wisdom Hacks
Interpretation over repetition.
Application over theory.